An Invitation to Friendship

From the Father's Heart
Volume II

CHARLES SLAGLE

Destiny Image®️ **Publishers, Inc.**
P.O. Box 310
Shippensburg, PA 17257-0310

"We Publish the Prophets"

ISBN 0-7684-2013-X

For Worldwide Distribution
Printed in the U.S.A.

This book and all other Destiny Image, Revival Press, and Treasure House books are available
at Christian bookstores and distributors worldwide.

For a U.S. bookstore nearest you,
call **1-800-722-6774**.
For more information on foreign distributors,
call **717-532-3040**.
Or reach us on the Internet:
http://www.reapernet.com

Dedication

There is nothing that brings me more joy than to dedicate this book to my wife, Paula Slagle. Not only is Paula my soul mate, the love of my life, and the mother of our son, Bryan, but she also is the gift God gave to me more than 30 years ago. And He did it within two months of my praying, "Lord, please send me the wife You have chosen for me. Please let her be beautiful inside and as well as 'out'—and let her also be my very best friend forever." God answered that prayer in the spring of 1968.

Since then, almost everything I have learned about unconditional love—committed love—has come through Paula. Muddling through the mundane for three decades; hanging on (often with white knuckles!) to God's promises in the face of discouragement that defies description; laying down her natural expectations of and from life to take Christ's life and hope to others; believing in her husband when he struggled to hope and believe but couldn't—this is the gift God has given me through my wife.

Some folks think that my understanding of our Father's heart of love is too radical—even verging on "heretical." My response? Maybe so. One thing I can say for sure is this: Since my heavenly Father has so faithfully loved me through Paula, I simply don't know how to think of Him except as being the Sheer Essence of Unfailing Love...Heavenly Yet Down-to-Earth Goodness Personified.

I'm not saying that God has always carried me around on a pink glory cloud, whispering soft comforts in my ear. Had He not become a *solid wall* to oppose my stubborn stupidity (oh so many times!), I would not be on planet Earth writing books!

Nor am I saying that Paula has devoted herself to being a sugary nice "angel" of the Christmas tree ornament variety. Some of the most loving things my wife has done for me did not seem loving to me when she said or did them! I must give her credit, though; Paula has been more consistently gentle, patient, and pleasant in her daily living than anyone I have ever met. No doubt she would challenge these words, but I would not write them if I did not know them to be true.

Now here is something to think about. Is it possible that my heavenly Father has given me a wife who loves me with deeper commitment than He does? *Ha!*

Paula and I pray that the Holy Spirit will anoint the contents of this book and open your eyes to see as never before your heavenly Father's heart of committed love. For God is Love, and Love means commitment.

Acknowledgments

God has revealed His heart of committed love to me through so many wonderful people. So first I want to express my gratitude for my heavenly Father and His unrelenting kindness. I now realize that He has shown me His kindness by first allowing me to learn what it is *not*.

During my childhood, my family and I learned of our heavenly Father and His Son, Jesus Christ, in a spiritual environment that, on the whole, was harsh, legalistic, and often frightening. In effect, the message was, "The Lord loves you, but, unless *you* line up—and pronto—He's out of here!"

I can remember many nights when, as a child, I lay awake crying as I struggled to remember *every* sin I had committed and begged God to forgive it. Perhaps many readers will be shocked and saddened to think that a little boy would live in horror of God and His (supposed) hopeless abandonment. But that was exactly my experience.

Furthermore, even now there are many children in the world whose inner picture of "God" is preparing them for a life of misery—and perhaps cynical agnosticism. Such children have no solid sense of *identity*. They have no deep and settled assurance of having a *good purpose for being*. And why? It is because of the religious "God-Picture" that their unwitting, if sincere, spiritual mentors have given them. I call it "religious" because Christianity is not about religion—man's efforts to search for, find, and appease an angry deity. Christianity is about God coming to us. It is about our Good Shepherd who searches for each one of His lost sheep *until* He finds it. Christianity is the "glad tidings of great joy" that our Savior-God has come to seek and to save that which was lost... to set the captives free! (See Matt. 12:18-21; Luke 2:11; 15:1-4; 19:10.)

With that in mind, I am praying that this book will fall into the hands of many hurting people whose inadequate inner picture of God has made it impossible for them to hope or to have a solid sense of identity. (Heavenly Father, You're on!)

The years between 1984 and 1996 have been the most revolutionary ones of my life. It was in that season that God in His (terribly wonderful) kindness "broke through" again and again until, at last, He utterly shattered my warped picture of Him. While our Good Father was pulverizing my false image (one worse than Moloch!) that called itself "God," He was doing the same thing in the lives of my dear family. Imagine how all of us emotionally "bounced off the walls" during those years! And I will admit, yours truly ricocheted off the walls more violently than any of my loved ones did. Yikes! A total "paradigm shift" was occurring. An utterly wrong foundation was being dynamited and removed from my life, and a completely new one was being laid down.

How grateful I am for the wonderful and lifelong friends through whom God nurtured us during that season! They have been not only a source of constant encouragement, but also literally His healing hands that have touched and shaped our lives over the years. Paula and I both are so thankful for them. (Dear ones, you *know* who you are.) But at this point

I would like to say a big thank you to those friends who have directly contributed to the composition of this book. And now, here goes....

(1) Thank you, Carolyn Barnett! Since 1984 you have invested literally countless hours of healing counsel and prayer into our lives. It was through you, dear Carolyn, that our heavenly Father first wrote us a "letter" (such as the ones this book contains) and began to reveal His true heart to us. I could say more—far more—to express my appreciation, but you would pounce on me "like a duck on a June bug" if I did!

(2) Thank you, Jayne Hover! Jayne, you worked as our office manager for 11 years and have been such a blessing and a dear and proven friend to us. You "translated" much of the journaling that now appears in this book from my scribbles and typed them with your very own hands.

(3) Thank you, Paula Slagle, my wonderful wife! I am so grateful for all of your editorial and secretarial labors, which have been many, many, many.

(4) Thank you, Neil Slagle (my dear friend and nephew), for all of your editorial assistance and hours of labor at the computer to help make this book possible. I don't know how I would have made the last leg of this journey without you!

(5) Thank you, Cliff Hawley, not only for your anointed—and awe-inspiring—artistry that permeates this book from cover to cover, but also for your proven friendship.

(6) Thank you, Arthur Eedle. Your taking time to speak into my life and answer my countless questions has definitely contributed directly to the writing of this book. Your input has blessed me immeasurably by helping me to perceive our heavenly Father's heart of love in all things, including His righteous judgments.

(7) Thank you, Jeff Hall, and all the editorial staff of Destiny Image for your good input. May God reward you for helping to ensure that the messages contained in this book make sense to more people than just myself!

Author's Note

Several distinctives will easily be seen by all who read this book. They are the following:

(1) Because many of the letters touch on more than one issue, they are not divided into chapter-like categories. These messages are intended to unveil various aspects of the Father's heart. They were not meant to be collections compiling a reference book for "problem solving" or to replace the "promise box." However, they are listed by titles to help the reader find his way.

(2) The portrayal of Father's wit, irony, and humor is shown abundantly in the Bible but, unfortunately, is seldom portrayed in other writings. This I am prayerfully attempting to rectify to some small degree. (See Num. 22:28; I Sam. 5–6; Prov. 17:14; Matt. 11:16-19; 23:24.)

(3) The letters are often addressed to "deliverers," "saviors," "conquerors," "liberators," and "freedom fighters." This is to remind the reader that our Dad takes seriously His call for the Body of Christ to continue the work of Jesus in the world. As Christ was in this world, so are we. And as Christ was sent to this world, so are we. (See Obad. 1:21; John 20:21; I John 4:17.)

(4) In seeking to motivate the reader to righteous choices, the letters appeal more to reason and good sense than to fear of coming judgment. Hence, the reader may find phrases that sound a little odd (coming from God) cropping up. "In My view," "I think,"

and "the way I see it" are examples of this. This is to show that our Dad is always seeking to help us view things as He views them—to see as He sees. He knows that when we begin to see as He sees, think as He thinks, and feel as He feels, we will find ourselves strongly motivated to act as He acts. The Scriptures tell us to copy (emulate and mimic) our heavenly Father as His dearly beloved children. (See Isa. 1:18; Eph. 5:1; Col. 1:9-10.)

(5) The reader will note that many of the letters are signed "Dad." This is what "Abba, Father" literally means in the Scriptures. The Bible clearly teaches us that Father God longs to relate to each of His children on intimate, family terms. (See Rom. 8:15-17.)

(6) The capitalization of pronouns (Us, We, Our, Ours) that include the Divine Person with the reader is a respectful and affectionate reference to the reader's royal status as Father's child. Our Father longs to elevate our viewpoint concerning our relationship with Him.

On the other hand, all references to satan are purposely not capitalized, unless they occur at the beginning of a sentence. By this I am seeking to contrast the diminished power and significance of our enemy against the might and authority of our God and His children. (See Isa. 14:12-16; Rom. 8:15-17; Eph. 1:15-23; I Pet. 2:9-10.)

(7) The verb form "I AM" is consistently capitalized when spoken by Father. This is the name of our God, and it is emphasized to remind the reader of His unchanging love, power, and faithfulness. (See Ex. 3:13-14.)

The messages that now have become the body of this book began as a series of "letters" from Father to me. In time, as these personal letters began to accumulate, I became sensitive to the fact that our Lord desired that I share them with others.

Only the Bible is infallibly inspired by God. The messages in this book are not prophecies, *per se.* I am fully aware that our Father may choose to give them a personal, prophetic impact to some readers on occasion, but no special inspiration is claimed. However, I pray that the words of this book will prove helpful for other "weary warriors" who seek to increasingly know our Father's heart. Obviously, these messages are intended to comfort the reader with the same comforts by which we, the Slagles, have also been comforted. (See II Cor. 1:3-7.)

Introduction

Have you ever met someone whom you liked immediately? Someone whom you instinctively knew you'd enjoy having as a friend—someone with whom you wanted to simply spend time and share your heart? Such a one didn't have to do anything in particular to win you over—you just knew that you would love to be friends.

Over these last few years we have learned that *that* is exactly how our heavenly Father feels about us. He has even allowed the backdrop of our own failures, shortcomings, and disappointments to showcase His intense love for us and His passionate desire to call us "friends." Just as *He* chose to come to Adam and Eve in the garden, before *and* after their sin, just as *He* called Abraham "the friend of God," just as Jesus told His disciples that *He* called them no longer servants, but friends—that is how God has loved us, reached out to us, and invited us into friendship with Himself. It is God reaching out to us, not the other way around.

It doesn't matter where you are in life, whether things are going well or going poorly. It isn't important whether you think you are living up to all the "expectations" of others or even those expectations you've imposed upon yourself. The only thing that matters is that He who is the "Lover of your soul" is calling you to come—to be His friend.

In 1989, the first book in this series, *From the Father's Heart*, was published. Since that time we have been so blessed to receive countless reports of lives being touched and changed by the "letters" in that book. May the same be true for this edition. No one knows better than Charles and myself that it is the anointing of the Holy Spirit that does the work. It is encouraging and humbling, all at the same time, to be part of that process.

As time passes, we all continue to grow and learn. The more time we spend with our heavenly Father, the more we understand of His nature and ways. And one of the biggest lessons we learn is that He truly wants us to be His friend. It is our prayer that the messages on these pages will cause you to know that the Father is issuing that same invitation to you, now, today—and forever.

His friend and yours,
Paula Slagle

An Invitation to Friendship

From the Father's Heart
Volume II

WHAT I WANT MOST
Matt. 7:11-12; I Cor. 13

*I*nquiring Child,

Life without Love... Is it possible? I have never thought so. What do you think? Some of My children think I AM narrow-minded and old-fashioned in this matter and they have set out to prove Me wrong.

I will tell you what I think. If you never learn anything else, what I want most for you is that you learn to love. In loving and truly caring about others you will acquire a wisdom that will never fade with your years. Riches will come to you that no earth-wealth can rival, and—best of all—you will be happy.

Are you amazed that God wants you to be happy? Why shouldn't I? I AM the Best Friend you will ever have!

Yours With Infinite Joy,
Your Real Dad

loquent Liberator,

I chuckle as I say this, but what are you telling Me that I do not already know? All of your deepest longings lie open before Me. When you cease talking, I will speak. Meanwhile your monologue is delaying Our dialogue. Don't misunderstand Me, child. I AM not unhappy that you are pouring out your heart to Me. I just want you to know that I AM here for you, and that I care, and that you *can* hear Me speaking inside you—when you are ready.

You have asked that I not let you stray from My will. I AM answering your prayers. So why do you fret? I AM granting you wisdom, protection and guidance, as per your request. Now, what do *you* want? Think about it. I'll be delighted to help you survey your options—in detail. Do you fear hearing My heart? You shouldn't. When did I ever abuse or deprive you? Again, child, all I AM doing is answering your prayers. Whatever you choose to do, I assure you that you will be glad later on that you took time to become quiet in My Presence.

No, I AM not annoyed. Not at all. When I created you I knew that sometimes you would be a bit...challenging? I love everything about you.

Your Devoted Father

YOU WILL SHINE
Ex. 33:18; II Cor. 3:7-18

herished Seeker,

I have heard your prayers, so be assured—you will shine! Without conscious thought you will literally transmit the healing radiance of My Glory. Just abide in My loving nurture and Presence. You do not need mere facts and information; what you need is Who I AM. Yes, you'll have to think about that, won't you?

Good! Meditate on it. That simple truth is the secret to untold riches, in light of which mere money will appear as refuse. Moses yearned that I show him the glory of My infinite goodness, and I rejoiced to fulfill his desire—freely. Do I show favoritism? Do I love My servant Moses more than I love you? Certainly not! He wrestled with frailties just as you do. Even so, I delighted to reveal Myself to him merely because he desired that I do so. He longed to know Me, just as you yearn to know Me.

As I was with Moses, so I will be with you, treasured conqueror. I have chosen you to liberate not just a few people, but many. You will unshackle multitudes from the agonizing bonds of despair and shame. This will happen not by your straining to assert yourself, but because you simply enjoy the benefits of My Glory—My life-transforming Presence that dwells inside you. Seek, and you will find. Knock, and the door will open to you. All who seek will find, and all who knock will gain entry to Unspeakable Joy.

Yours Faithfully, and With All Power,
Your Devoted Father

ALL OF MY LIFE
Ps. 91; Eph. 3:14-20

*T*rusted Nurturer,

Yes, I have taught you well. Thank you for holding fast to that which is good—and for your generosity in sharing with others all that I have lavished on you. However, you are now beginning to realize that what I have taught you is not enough. It is true, weary one. What you know has value only as it leads you to enter into Who I AM and into experiencing the wonder of who I AM shaping you to be.

You have asked, "Why do I still worry so much?" I will tell you. You need love, not just correct concepts about it. You need hope—solid and real hope—not mere explanations as to why it is possible. There will never come a time when Love will fail. People fail, but I never do. My Only Begotten Son came to help and to heal failing people. Have you forgotten? As long as you imagine that I want you to be miserable, you will be. You will never love Me, nor will you ever trust Me wholeheartedly, until you *know* that I love you more—far more—than you love Me.

I AM Unfailing Holy Love. Until Unfailing Holy Love becomes all in all—everything in everyone everywhere—pain will persist in your world. Therefore, the more My Essence saturates your being, the more deeply you will know contentment. I created you for My delight. Do you remember? You were made for Infinite Joy!

Enter in, child. Taste and see! Perfect Love casts out all fear. Worry will vanish! All problems will lose their power to harass you in the Secret Place of the

Most High. Treasured child, why should I be angry for having waited for you? I have waited for you all of My life!

With Deepest Joy,
Your Father

RUBBING OFF EFFECT
Deut. 7:22; Ps. 34:5

*S*earching One,

As you have noticed, I never rush. Nor am I ever bored (except with religious affairs), and I never feel nervous or tense. The longer We walk and talk together, and the more you allow Me to embrace you and enjoy your company, the less nervous and tense you will be. More and more you will become as I AM. You will increasingly think as I think, feel as I feel, and live as I live. That is My commitment to you. You can count on it.

The constant and gentle impact of My Presence on your life has a "rubbing off effect." The more you are exposed to My Essence, the more My nature rubs off on you. Little by little and bit by bit, Who I AM frees you to become who you are—who you actually are. But this process *must* occur gradually, here a little, there a little.

A doctor doesn't use an atomic bomb to perform radiation therapy. Such treatment would annihilate his patient, not heal him. So aren't you glad that I AM not in a hurry? You can relax now. I AM your Physician, and I will not fail. And neither will you. It is not going to happen. So you may as well choose not to worry.

I AM like the sign you have seen written on the rear of those large transport trucks that says: *I may be slow, but I am ahead of you.*

Chosen conqueror, mere words cannot describe how much I enjoy your company.

Dad

LOOK FOR ME
Rom. 12; Eph. 2:8-9; 3:14

S on,

Thank you for your passion to love and serve others even when they do not notice or show appreciation. Rejoice in My Love. Spend the rest of this day basking in My enjoyment of you. In childlike trust, look for Me in all, and you will see Me in all. You will see Me in all situations, all events, all encounters.

Haven't I promised that if you grow weary or stumble I will never forsake you? I have recently shown you, yet again, that your security does not depend on your own energy, wisdom or efforts. It is My power that sustains, guides and protects you. Always!

The reason I ask you to obey Me is that I want you to savor *every* joy and succeed in *every* good venture. However, you cannot wholeheartedly obey Me as long as you labor under the illusion that your obedience is what determines My commitment to you. That is the lie of conditional love. As long as you believe that lie, despair and frustration will dominate your life. True Righteousness arrives—and thrives—in an environment of joy. Focusing on problems will never free you from their power. Redirect your focus, treasured conqueror, toward Someone Who loves you far more than you can imagine ...

Your Devoted Father

WHAT I SAY GOES
Ps. 12:5-7; 130; Rom. 8:38-39; I John 4:18

𝓗urting Child,

I have come so that your fears will go away. Perfect Love... that is My name. In My Presence no fear can survive. Our being together now is no coincidence. Those lies luring you into despair are satanic. Reject them! That which is Holy inspires hope. Our enemy accuses and slanders. He is the one who trumps up fictitious scenarios to torment your mind. It is he who seeks to paralyze you. Why? That wicked one knows the power you wield. He knows the Divine Energy that surges inside you, which you have yet to discover. So of course he invents designs to derail you! That is why in your mind's eye your small flaws loom larger than life. That is exactly the accuser's plan, isn't it? He wants *your* frailties—which have yet to be healed—to seem larger than *My* life.

Nonsense! Nothing is larger than I AM. Nothing! Furthermore, why should I want you to be consumed with self-loathing and driven by fear? Hear Me, treasured one. That is exactly what I do *not* want. What I want with all of My Being is for you to feel secure in My love.

You will never know the true fear of the Lord until you understand that mercy motivates all that I do. You will never trust Me until you know I AM trustworthy. Your heart will reverence and hold Me in deepest honor *only* when you know that you can count on Me—no matter what.

I have promised to defend you, have I not? So here I AM! I know you feel helpless. Your sorrow is ever before Me. Be assured, child. Even now I AM dismantling all evil devices. Soon they will unravel before your very eyes, and you and I will laugh and sing together as they do! Consider the song of My psalmist, David: "The words of the Lord are flawless, like silver refined in a furnace...seven times."

David is right. My promises are imperishable! They are as solid as eternity. They are as secure as I AM. Do you understand what that means? It means, what I say goes! No force in creation can stop it, for it is My Word that sustains the worlds.

When you were younger you loved astronomy. You were a devoted stargazer. Yes, how well I recall. We have much in common, you and I. Stargazing happens to be one of My own favorite pastimes. Do you still thrill as you remember those supernovas that are exploding in multi-colored splendor? I know how you have yearned for a closer view of those pulsating quasars I posted to blink on the circular brink of infinity. And one day you shall have it.

I know also how My vast, cosmic meadows of galaxies captivate your imagination. In the daydreams of your youth you lived there more often than you lived on earth. Your loved ones were always having to call you down from the far reaches of your journeys into interstellar infinity and remind you of lunch. But even then, while others chatted and ate, your mind returned to explore the constellations.

Oh yes. I know all about you, and I AM glad you love My starry heavens. And, chosen conqueror, not only are they Mine, they are also yours. I created them all for your joy. My Word called them forth. I merely spoke, and the cosmos burst into being! It was just that simple. Hardly anyone believes it these days, but that is exactly what happened. What I say goes!

My dear child, if I can breathe a universe into existence with a mere word, why should you worry about your tomorrows? I will complete the good work I have begun in you. I AM your Father. You will and must become as I AM. Nothing ever can or ever will separate you from My love. You are Mine, and I AM yours. You ride on the strong shoulders of the Lion of Judah. I will continue to remind you of this as We approach the end of this small conflict.

Remember, this battle *is* Mine. What I say goes!

Your Omnipotent Father

SOON YOU WILL KNOW
II Sam. 14:14; Ps. 27:13-14; Rom. 5:7-11

estless Child,

Never fear, I AM here. I realize you are a bit wobbly at the moment. I know you find it difficult to distinguish between My voice and the thoughts of your own mind. Rest assured, My love for you is tender, and My compassion is fathomless and unfailing. That is why I bless even your most faltering steps. I know exactly where you are right now. In fact, I AM more aware of your position than you are. Even now I AM reaching out to you where you are in order to bring you to where I AM. Will you meditate on this truth? It will greatly encourage you. The little god that religiosity advertises gives impatiently, with grudging reluctance. That is not the God of the glad tidings of great joy, and it is not Who I AM!

Immortality... That is your destiny, dear child. My offspring will live forever. They will outlast the constellations! I know that some people would have you believe that you can count on Me... *only* if I can count on you. What nonsense! You were counting on yourself more than you trusted in My power *before* My Spirit awakened your heart to know Me.

Why would I send you a message that would catapult you back into the despair of that dark era? Religious minds are always setting deadlines. I AM Limitless Love, and I AM always extending lifelines.

I will not disappoint you. In your heart you have heard My Spirit whispering, "Seek the face of your Father," have you not? Then do so! Wait in My healing Presence with quiet joy. I will not hide My glory from you. I will not shun you in anger. Holding grudges is not in My nature. I AM your constant Helper and your devoted Friend. I will never desert you. No earthly father or mother could love you as I do. You will always find acceptance with Me. And always means always!

Soon, cherished one, you will know My heart and My ways. You already walk in the path of My miraculous provision, or haven't you noticed? So be assured! I will expose every lie that any enemy utters. No harm will befall you. Not only will you savor the aroma of My Presence, you will constantly exude My fragrance. Furthermore, you will live in the *substance* of My glory and goodness.

After all, that is why I created you! That is your purpose for being.

Yours With Infinite Joy,
Father

SOMETHING WONDERFUL
Gal. 1:10

*W*eary-Hearted Child,

Not everyone shares My tastes. So of course not everyone is going to like you! Many people dislike Me. Even I cannot please all people at all times. I AM Truth. I AM Reality Personified. Reality *cannot* please unhappy souls as long as they prefer to live a lie. It simply is not possible. Consider yourself to be in Good Company, because you are!

Make it your policy to love your fellow human beings, but to practice only what I will always applaud. You already enjoy My approval and acceptance, so you can love others without fretting about whether or not they appreciate you or understand your heart.

Even in unfallen worlds the finite creatures that inhabit them do not possess the ability to understand hearts as I do. I should know, shouldn't I? Are you aware that Heaven's angels even now applaud you from many realms in Our house? You have done well, treasured one. Enter into Joy Everlasting! I AM here, so do you mind doing it now?

I led you into difficulties to show you something wonderful. You needed to learn how My love can conquer in the midst of chaos. Child, you *are* learning, I AM happy to report. When you comfort others in days to come, it will be My healing words that flow from your well-trained spirit. You will not make mere nice-sounding noises, devoid of My life and My power.

I AM so delighted with your progress!

Love Always,
Dad

YOUR SOURCE OF SECURITY
Ps. 4:8; Isa. 43:18-19; 48:10,17

*F*earless Freedom Fighter,

You have been tested in the furnace of affliction. But forget the past. I AM doing a new thing. Haven't you observed it? Even now, it springs forth for Our joy! You need to hear this again, so I don't mind repeating Myself. I AM your Deliverer, your Protector, your God. Above all else, I AM your loving Father. I *enjoy* teaching you. It is My delight to guide your steps. I have promised you many times that I would enlighten you with My wisdom and shield you from harm, have I not? So forsake frenzy, child of My heart. Choose to rest in My love and enter into joy. You can count on Me. I will instruct you. When you need it, the "light" will come on inside you, and you *will* know the way you should go.

Why do I not inform you in advance of the details of situations you are facing? The reason is quite simple. If I did, your weary mind would only have more words to misconstrue. As you've already discovered, the situations themselves are always far easier than the thoughts you entertain about them beforehand. Besides, you have yearned for simplicity, haven't you? So I AM fulfilling the desires of your heart. Savor sleep and relish rest, valiant warrior. I AM your Source of Security. You need nothing else.

We both know that.

With All My Love,
Your Almighty Father

THEN...
Ps. 66; Rom. 1:21; Eph. 2:5-12; Jas. 1:18

 ear Child,

Ingratitude... You have experienced the pain of others not appreciating your sincere efforts and hard labors, haven't you? I just want you to know that I understand, and I care. All I ask is that you not let the ingratitude of another person poison your heart with bitterness. A bitter heart is a thankless one. Why let Our enemy throw a party in celebration of how he succeeded in stealing your song?

A satanic lie... That is what caused ingratitude to fill the hearts of Adam and Eve. As a result, My true glory became distorted in their thinking, as well as in the minds of all their offspring—but you already know the rest of the story. Even so, are you aware that My Son Light Who is the Living Truth is working a plan? Absolutely! He plans to *refill* with jubilant song all the sons and daughters of Adam and Eve.

One day every knee shall bow in deepest adoration, and every tongue will acclaim Christ and *give joyful thanks* for His Lordship! A lie brought the curse of ingratitude and destruction. The Living Truth— even now—by the power of His cross, is at work to reverse that satanic curse, so that thanksgiving resounds as the cosmic theme once again!

While I AM on that subject, I want to thank you for pioneering to reestablish grateful song in the earth! You are a pacesetter, a kind of "firstfruits" in My plan for My cherished creation, dear child. And We both know that Heaven's Reign has to begin *somewhere*, don't you agree? I so appreciate your allowing it to begin in you.

Today I have dropped in to remind you that you *can* perceive Heaven governing in all things. Yes, even at this moment I make all things new. You can see that, if you will view everything through My eyes. And you will see through My eyes if you want to, child. Only say yes, and you *shall* behold and enjoy!

Then...you no longer will struggle and strive to produce faith, for faith does not come from parroting positive platitudes. Assurance of My love—that is what fosters faith. Faith *functions* by love. You have thought much about Me, and I appreciate that. But now, will you commune with Me heart to heart? I long to hold you.

Yours Truly,
Father

MY GRAND DESIGN
Isa. 55:8-11; Matt. 6:10; I Cor. 1:20

*T*roubled Child,

You have prayed for My will to be done on earth just as it is in Heaven. Have you forgotten? I haven't. When you ask for anything that harmonizes with My heart's aspirations, you can rest assured that I hear you and that you have what you desire of Me.

As I have told you, My thoughts are not your thoughts. Your ways cannot begin to compare with the wisdom of Mine. As the heavens reach above the earth into infinity, so My ways are higher than yours. My reasoning astounds the most astute of human minds. Aren't you glad? You should be! My wisdom has saved you from many a snare, treasured one.

I will not disappoint you. Even now My Spirit is working in the midst of the seeming contradictions in your life, shaping them to conform to My loving purposes. At the same time you are learning to trust in My power. It is easy to tell others that you serve a God of miracles, isn't it? However, sooner or later situations will arise that demand that you *show* people what you have been telling them. At this very moment My Spirit is preparing you for such adventures.

Do you really think I have led you this far to toss you on the scrap heap? Cease fretting about your failures and living in fear of future ones. I saw your weaknesses long before I flung the galaxies from My fingers. Your mistakes are already accounted for, child. I AM weaving My grand design for your destiny around them.

Believe in your Anointing. I do!

Loving You Always,
Father

YOU "SHALL" BE HAPPY
Matt. 7:9-12; I Pet. 1:13-22

L ovable Liberator,

No good father would demand that his child do the impossible. So when I tell you to be holy in all you do and say, I AM not demanding that you instantly perfect yourself. Far less do I desire that "thou shouldest speak" and appear as though you somehow had managed to travel through time from the 1600's into now.

Long-faced religiosities who make it a point to wear old-fashioned clothes and to strut about scowling at other people have missed My point completely. Holiness is not weirdness! It is a pity that many minds have muddled *sanctification* and *sanctimony* together as synonymous terms. Don't you agree?

When I call you into holiness, I AM inviting you into wholeness, the wholeness that emerges from Our friendship—from Our walking and talking together. Another reason I yearn for you to shine with the radience of My purity is that I want others to experience My Healing Essence as *you* touch them. I long that you and I intoxicate everyone everywhere with the wine of Real Love—Authentic Love—so they become irreversibly addicted.

Furthermore, I yearn for your happiness. Do you realize that unless you are maturing so that you increasingly reflect My true glory, you will never be happy? Believe Me! I know what it takes to make you happy, for I AM the Happy God. Therefore, you "shall" be happy because I AM. That is My commitment to you. Are you surprised? I don't mind telling you again: I have no interest whatsoever in religiosity! I AM interested in you.

Thanks for taking time for Us.

Yours With Joyful Anticipation,
Father

THESE MOMENTS OF WAITING
Gen. 16; 21; Ps. 37:4-6; Heb. 10:35

*I*nquiring Child,

Why do you look to books or to other human beings for guidance? You are wrong to imagine that I prefer the company of My other children over yours. Shhh! Listen, cherished one. To your ears I may be speaking softly, but I AM speaking. I AM not distanced from you by light-years of cosmic infinity; I dwell inside you. I enjoy you! Nothing pleases Me more than to be your Friend and constantly make Myself available to you.

The more your heart becomes convinced that I love you, the less you will worry about straying from My will. Committed friends tend to share the same interests, the same high aspirations. As a result, their hearts lead them toward the same goals. How much more is this true where you and I are concerned. Our love-bond makes you heir to unlimited power!

So, child, why waste these moments of waiting with worry? Abraham fathered Ishmael in an attempt to hasten My plan of giving him a son. Do you recall? Even so, in due time, I gave him Isaac, the son of My promise. Centuries later I sent My angel Gabriel to inform aged Zechariah that his elderly wife, Elizabeth, would bear him a son. He balked in unbelief when he first heard of My radical plan. So, for a season he lost the use of his tongue. However, little John the Baptist *was* born. Years later he became the world's greatest prophet and paved the way for the coming Messiah.

Consider! Abraham blundered ahead of My plan while Zechariah lagged behind. Nevertheless, I fulfilled

My word to them both, did I not? So it will be with you, chosen conqueror! Be at peace concerning My process and your part in it. I AM! Should you need any adjustment, I will tell you, never fear. In fact, not only will I tell you, I also will help you! Haven't I always?

Thank You for Trusting,
Your Devoted Father

MY FINGER CARVED A PATH
Luke 4:18-30; John 10:18

*H*urting One,

Yes, I have called you to follow Christ as He continues to pour out His life in self-giving love. Even so, I have *not* called you to become a doormat under the grinding heels of the ruthless. Offering your life to Me moment by moment as a loving sacrifice is one thing. Submitting to sadism is a different matter entirely!

Did David allow demented Saul to impale him with a spear, or did he dodge it? In Nazareth did Jesus submit to a crazed mob and allow them to hurl Him from a cliff? Read for yourself: "He walked right through the crowd and went on His way."

How did He manage that feat? Your Lord submitted to Me. He did *not* submit to murderers. So just as I had once parted the Red Sea, My finger carved a path through the crowd that sought to destroy Him. I delivered My dear Son from His enemies! Thus your Good Shepherd was able to say, "No one takes My life. I lay it down when I choose."

Child, you can trust Me to grant you the same power. It breaks My heart when My unwitting children submit to self-appointed spiritual guides who abuse them. Why do they submit? They do so *simply because* their abusers have brainwashed them to believe that I require it! Wives endure violence and children suffer untold agony—all because confused people have taught them that My holiness demands it.

Not so! If that were true, I would not have rescued My people Israel from their cruel captors in Egypt. Nor would I have instructed the mother of baby

Moses to hide him from Pharaoh, who had issued a death warrant against him.

Please hear Me, hurting one. I AM a God of mercy. When will all of My children believe this? Cling to Me. As I have told you, making ways where there are none is My specialty.

Yours With Deepest Compassion,
Father

RESPECTABILITY
Matt. 12:18-21; Gal. 3:8,17

*B*ewildered Child,

I will never desert you. It is not in My nature to abandon hurting people. My love-covenant is not based on your success or performance; it is founded on My unfailing mercy.

"What on earth is happening?" you have asked. I AM training you to trust. That is what is happening. I know that you face many obstacles in your journey toward wholeness, and you are right. I have not removed some of your more disreputable-looking flaws by a sovereign act of My power. If I had, you would have become blind to your need for My tender mercy. You would have imagined that you somehow had managed to earn My love. By confusing the world's idea of respectability for "godliness," you would have settled for far less than My best.

I AM not in the business of reproducing replicas of the world's stereotypical success images. Far less am I interested in manufacturing religious robots. The world is overrun by too many of them already! Don't you agree? I have no use for such facsimiles, as well-rounded and nice as they may appear to be. I AM spawning a new race, a reigning family of co-deliverers who are radiant with My glory. I AM forming a company of compassionate restorers who reflect the True Light of My Son Jesus Christ!

Never fear, chosen one. My Son will not fail or become discouraged. Your Strong Deliverer *will* labor on until He has established full deliverance in that awesome, if tiny, bit of earth called "you." I have destined you to become like Him! Because your Elder Brother and I have borne patiently with your frailties, compassion will crown your ministry.

Things were possessing you. That is why I took them away—not permanently, but just for a season. I AM making use of these days to remove all impurities in your deepest self that have brought you pain. These toxic elements are the result of your confusing Our enemy's lies for the truth. But never fear! All will be well. The feelings of paranoia you are experiencing are normal. They are not your fault. They usually accompany withdrawal. Interestingly, you will find yourself more at peace from this point on. I know how your personality functions!

Cherished one, when you know what is happening, it is easier to be happy, isn't it? It is not impossible to be happy when you are not "in the know," but that is a lesson you will enjoy later on. For now, pursue love, laughter—and life. The whole reason I disentangled you from all of that exhausting paraphernalia was to free you to breathe and to enjoy life—Real Life! Only in the midst of Life's enjoyment can you discover the "real you." You've spent enough time struggling to be a facsimile—a silly hodgepodge of "everyone else's" ideas.

Consider yourself rescued! You are. You are Mine and deeply loved. Thank you for trusting!

Your Mighty Fortress,
Abba Father

WITH FLYING COLORS
Luke 10:25-37

aring Explorer,

Surprise! Here I AM again, assuring you that I AM greater than your keen intellect. I have all kinds of interesting ways of cropping up, don't I?

What! Me give up on the Church? You must be joking. As for organized religiosity, as you well know, that is something I have never endorsed! So how could I give up on something I never had anything to do with in the first place? I have no intention of ever giving up on the world, so there is no way I will ever give up on the Church. That is because, in its purest essence, the Church is made up of radical rescuers like yourself. Such individuals detest religious hypocrisy while they yearn to lavish healing love on marginalized and suffering people. The Church—the true Body of Christ—is dedicated to bringing deliverance to the lost and displaced of the world, while organized religion aspires to escape the world and "go to Heaven." My radical restorers yearn for Love's desire to be fully accomplished on earth just as it is in Heaven. No offense intended, but I think you need to familiarize yourself a bit more with the Bible.

Are you aware that I love agnostics and atheists? Many of these are "good Samaritans" and are among the most honest people I know. They are not afraid to ask hard questions. They refuse to pretend reverence toward abuse that parades itself as "spirituality." Many who question My existence come through with flying colors when it comes down to what is dear to My heart: *actually helping people.* You and I are better friends than you know!

I was just thinking of Jesus... How much honest investigating have you done regarding His claims? I couldn't resist asking. By the way, I interpret all heart longings as prayers. So be prepared for a few notable miracles. I know how desperately you need them.

> With Deepest Understanding,
> Your Real Dad

THE DAY WILL COME
Eph. 4:21-32; 5:1; I Cor. 13:12

*9*nquiring Restorer,

I don't mind repeating Myself. So again, holiness means wholeness. It is wholeness, resplendent with the radiance of My glory and heart-purity. How deeply I desire that for you! Why? I think you deserve it. I created you in My image and called you good, long before you awakened to life in this world.

I AM called Good. Therefore, holiness is your destiny. Without it, no person ever can or ever will see Me. Those who are not whole lack the clarity of vision to perceive and appreciate love. And, of course, Love—Unfailing Pure Love—is Who I AM. That is why you must beware of bitterness, child of My heart.

Which is more important—what people have done to you and for you? Or what Christ has done for you and in you? Only ask, and I will open your eyes to see! You are not wrong to want everyone to love and understand you. The day will come when they will. For now, though, you must bear in mind that even the most spiritually sensitive human beings see as "through a glass, darkly." So your priority must be receiving My love and giving it away. If you make it your priority to influence other people to understand and love you, you will only break your own heart.

We both think it is right that everyone should love everyone. Yet for that to happen it has to begin with someone. Can you think of anyone?

I AM so blessed having you in My life!

Your Devoted Father

STOP NITPICKING
Phil. 3:12

*T*reasured One,

You gave what you had. So will you please stop nitpicking with your past? After you gave what you had, I gave what I had. So I more than made up for your lack.

Since then I have expanded your reserves. You now enjoy greater riches, and you will possess even more to give in days to come. However, when increased abundance arrives, you mustn't look back and criticize what you gave today by comparing it to what you acquired later on. Such negative analysis only wounds your heart and causes My Gentle Spirit to grieve for you. My Spirit longs to encourage you, child. Keeping you running scared and glancing back over your shoulder is *not* Heaven's agenda!

You will be far happier once the truth comes home to your heart that My sufficiency and your seeming insufficiency are separate subjects entirely. Is it any wonder that you have felt spread so thin? Your trying to be "God" (the Everlasting Fountain of Supply) for everyone else is the culprit. Repent!

Yours Smiling,
Dad

THE SOLID CERTAINTY
Isa. 61; II Cor. 4:18

*V*aliant Conqueror,

Knowing... possessing knowledge that is deep, settled, and unshakable... That is better than having a feeling. Feelings are untrustworthy and fleeting. Feelings can fool you and lead you astray. Faith, however, that springs from the *solid certainty* that I love you will propel you into astonishing feats of power!

Such faith has nothing to do with feelings. Child, you are too old to scrutinize your emotions and look for odd sensations. I have crowned you with My wisdom! You have the mind of Christ. Your anointing shatters prison doors and heals broken hearts! Walk in it. Trust in it. My Spirit will not disappoint you.

You learned this truth long ago, but lately I have been helping you to review it again. Why? You already know why, but I don't mind telling you what you already know. Promotion demands preparation. I AM promoting you to perform new exploits of power, just as I promised you earlier. So I have chosen first to show you the strength of the faith-foundation that I have established inside you. That discovery will empower you to launch out, laughing in the face of fear!

Now go. Go with the confidence of a conqueror! You might as well, treasured one, because that is what you are!

With Deepest Confidence,
Your Dad

ANY MESSAGE FROM "GOD"
John 6:63; I Thess. 5:20-21

My Dear Child,

The words I speak are breath and life! Why should I harass you with sudden rebukes and addle you with surprise assignments spoken through someone else? You constantly make yourself available to Me. Am I not able to address you personally? Any "message from God" that ignores Our previous discussions and responds to your penitent tears with pompous threats is a hoax.

Some of My less seasoned prophets have yet to learn the difference between their opinions and Mine. When My Spirit enlightens them to see a thing, they assume that, having seen it, they understand it. They confuse knowledge for wisdom. At other times, a man who seeks to convey My word to another fails to understand that I intended that message for *him*. Even so, child, I encourage you not to become cynical about prophecy. Simply test all things and hold fast to that which is good. And please... stay in touch with the good sense of humor I have given you! Ninety percent of spiritual discernment is resident within that gift.

Thank You for Listening,
Dad

NOSE-TO-NOSE
Isa. 25:7-9; John 14; Rev. 21:3-5

*S*earching and Treasured Child,

I AM Love, and Love never fails. That means Love never gives up—not ever. That also means you are in for an exhausting trip when you try to bail out and do your own thing, or haven't you noticed?

Welcome back! The reason you bailed out was because you imagined that your Good Shepherd and I wanted to be happy at your expense. As you recall, that is the same silly lie the serpent told Adam and Eve. "God wants to keep *you* groveling in stupidity while He enjoys all the benefits of boundless knowledge!" satan whined. However, you already know how the story goes after that, don't you?

Today I want to reaffirm Our friendship and remind you of My commitment to you. Your Lord said, "If anyone loves Me, he will keep My word." So do you know what I AM committed to do? I AM committed to cause you to love Jesus Christ with a passion that boggles your mind and blessedly breaks your heart.

Never fear, I AM not planning any disasters for you. I plan to do what I have always been doing. I will continue ordering your circumstances so that you keep coming nose-to-nose with your loving Savior. What do you think of the recent rescues your Lord and I engineered on your behalf? Did they surprise you? Just to confirm again: Any interpretation of Scripture that represents Me as being less reliable and patient than an earthly father *has* to be wrong. Period!

That does not mean that living apart from My counsel and nurture is painless. You already know that, so I need not elaborate. In My embrace you will find healing. Let's enjoy being together.

All things new... That is My promise to My creation, treasured child, and it is My promise to you. Behold! I make *all* things new.

With Unfailing Power and Devotion,
Father

RESULTS RESULTING
Ps. 131; Isa. 41:10-16; Phil. 1:6

*T*reasured Restorer,

Yes, I know that people offer you only shoddy performance while they demand that which is most costly from you. Sadly, many who claim to follow Christ are among the most notorious perpetuators of that injustice. They want *your* best gifts and efforts. Yet they habitually look for ways to give you as little as possible.

But, child, you no longer labor under the tyranny of tit-for-tat legalism. You now realize that My love secures you and that you need nothing else. So I want to thank you for making every effort to live in the Light of My Son, your Good Shepherd. I AM trusting you to continue following Him as He pours out His life for self-serving people who are not easy to love.

These days you no longer strive in frenzy because you fear My hopeless abandonment. Such irrational religiosity no longer warps your perception of Who I AM and how I treat My little neighbors. Now it is hope and holy desire that spur you on to perform daring deeds of deliverance! My smallest wish is your command, because you have grown to cherish and trust Me for Who I AM.

Good! That is the kind of heart-submission I have yearned to see happen in you. Now you are free to love—truly love. So at this point We can get on with your life. Our life! Now We can establish irreversible victories.

I have not been ignoring your prayers, cherished one. Will you believe Me? As you well know, I can produce immediate results, but I refuse to specialize in them. If I did, neither you nor I nor anyone else would appreciate the results resulting from all of those lovely looking, instant "solutions."

Think about it. And while you are thinking, consider some of those forty-five-year-old spoiled brats you've had to put up with in your lifetime. Such people were nurtured in an environment where nearly all their demands were met immediately! Has getting what they wanted the moment they piped up for it turned them into happy people? You and I both know the answer to that. Do you enjoy their company? No? Neither do I. Nor does anyone else!

Thank you for trusting.

Yours With Devotion,
Father

THE SECRET
Rom. 12; Gal. 6:6-9

ear Servant-Hearted Child,

Brilliant! At last you are seeing the light. The secret to overcoming fear of people's opinions is to love them too much to care how they may feel about you. Do you now see why I have been keeping you so busy? These days you find it nearly impossible to focus on your inadequacies or on those of others.

I AM overjoyed by your progress! In getting out of yourself you are discovering My True Self and finding your true self as well. Thus you are learning to live a life of love. Personally, I can't think of a better way to live, can you?

I also want to thank you for bearing patiently with My leaders. One reason I brought you into their lives was to show them the power of unconditional love. One reason I brought them into your life was so that you may profit by learning from their mistakes. Aren't you glad I love and trust you so much?

Child, I have promised that you shall have no other gods before Me. As you have noticed, I AM fulfilling that promise! I keep giving you glimpses of the chinks in the armor of My servants—who also happen to be your would-be idols. I know that you understand why I do so. It is not to enable you to discourage or destroy them. Rather, I show you their frailties because I AM trusting you to cover and shield them with your love and your prayers. As you and I both know very well, it is love—not criticism and scorn—that covers a multitude of sins.

What a blessing you are!

Yours With Highest Esteem,
Father

THAT EXHAUSTING SYNDROME
Phil. 2:3-11

*D*espondent Child,

Self-pity is a sinister spirit, a tiny demon that speaks loudly of "justice." That wily spirit's ploy is to fill your heart with resentment, grief and rage. Why? Just to keep you miserable! That is why.

Have you forgotten? Self-pity always seduces its victim with the reasonable-sounding snares of respect, appreciation, and fairness. Then it whispers, "Are you receiving *your* dues?" The last response that little devil wants to hear from you is, "Perhaps not! But did Jesus receive His?" At all costs he must keep that line of reasoning from surfacing! It would utterly spoil his devious scheme to keep you shackled to the idolatry of human opinion.

I AM sending you this message because I know you are tired of that exhausting syndrome. Self-pity never brought you any joy, did it? It even failed to deliver its promised reward of "self-respect."

You have let other people declare your value. You have forgotten that in My sight you possess infinite value. Repent! Resume praying for an outpouring of My Spirit upon those whom I have called you to serve, and just keep being the blessing you are. Many thanks, and God be with you!

But of course, I AM!

Yours With Highest Esteem,
Dad

YOU WERE MY IDEA
Ps. 139

 reasured Child,

You need not try to convince Me. I know you cannot heal yourself. Your own efforts have failed because I alone can do this work. You are powerless within yourself, hurting one, and I don't expect you to perform the impossible! I only ask that you do one thing: Abide in My loving nurture.

If at times you find yourself unable to do that, just remember—I AM committed to you anyway. I will remove all obstacles and gently maneuver you into My healing Presence. Isn't that how I drew you to Myself in the first place? You have not chosen Me. I have chosen you, and you are worth *all* My labors of love.

I know your heart. I understand your frailty. I know your deepest desires and take into account every factor that contributes to your pain. I know you did not "choose" these factors. I know that many of them were already present when you arrived in this world. You certainly did not choose to be born!

No, you were *My* idea. That is why you are here! So will you rest in My love and stop reasoning? Will you turn your gaze from the past and walk on? You cannot successfully move forward and look backward at the same time. Turn around, child! Follow Me! Have you forgotten? That is what "repentance" means.

Yours With Everlasting Commitment,
Dad

DESPAIR'S CHILD
Ps. 34:4-5; Phil. 3:10-15

Sorrowful One,

I AM not your enemy. I love you, and I AM on your side. Nothing has changed between Us. So please, child, stop degrading yourself, will you? Human wrath cannot foster a climate where virtue can grow and flourish. Harboring anger toward self spawns only frustration, despair, and more failure.

Surely you have noticed by now that self-hatred fuels lust. Why? It destroys hope. That is why. In the absence of hope, irresponsible behavior erupts and mind-binding addictions begin to tyrannize and destroy. That is because despair's child is insanity; it can give birth to no other offspring.

Yes, godly sorrow does lead to repentance. I could not agree more. After all, My Spirit authored those words. However, I must protest that there is nothing godly about groveling in self-loathing and remorse! That is not at all what I have in mind for you; My heart yearns for something far better.

Hurting one, let Us embrace. I long to hold you close and to flood your aching heart with joy. Remember! My wrath lasts but for a moment. So child, why do you extend your anger beyond the boundaries of Mine? All victories and all virtues spring from Our fellowship, not from your fury or frenzy. That is what Paul meant when he said that when you walk in the Spirit, you will not fulfill the desires of the flesh. The more you learn how to love (and I AM here to teach you), the less you will desire anything that is contrary to My highest aspirations for you.

Thank you for listening.

Yours With Deepest Understanding,
Father

THE OUTCOME
Ps. 18:25-27

*L*onely Liberator,

Thank you for trusting Me—come what may and no matter what. I just want to confirm that yes, I allowed you to experience treachery at the hands of My wayward children. I trusted you in that trial. It was not to punish you, but to train you to recognize what ministry is not—and what love is not. Now you know how *not* to treat the hurting people I will entrust into your care in days to come. And of course, knowing how not to deal with My wounded ones, you now see all the more clearly how you *are* to nurture and love them.

Will you please be at peace about your public image? I AM! Rest assured, the coming flood tide of My favor on you will astonish everyone, including your detractors! They will be shocked into silence, and I will break their hard hearts. One by one, they will come to you weeping, and they will ask for your forgiveness. Do you doubt My ability to devise such events? You shouldn't! I have vindicated you before.

I also have brought you down a few notches on occasions, have I not? (I always enjoy seeing you smile!) Oh yes, I know how to vindicate the humble and bring low the lofty. As you well know, to the pure I show Myself pure and to the deceptive and self-serving I show Myself shrewd. I know how to deal with people of every kind! Cherished one, will you continue to trust Me? The time will come when those who hurt you will love and treasure you as I do. Meanwhile, I AM shutting the mouths of "the lions."

Rest! Sleep, wounded warrior. Allow Me to fight your battles. You will like the outcome. I promise!

Forever Your Strong Fortress,
Father

A POSITION OF HONOR
Isa. 11:1-4; Rom. 15:1-13

Committed Conqueror,

I know it is difficult, but please continue to sow the seeds of mercy. I want you to reap their harvest. Refuse to jump to conclusions based on what your physical eyes see or what your natural ears hear. Resolve to allow My Spirit to teach you, and judge nothing before the appointed time. That includes judging yourself, treasured one.

I have placed you in a position of honor, a position of trust. I have chosen you to bear the burdens of those who are weak. You know why, don't you? I do. I know the strength I have deposited in your life. So I have placed you where you are, to love the unlovely.

I know you remember how I loved you into wholeness when you were despair-ridden and broken. I dealt tenderly with your frailties, did I not? Yes, I was merciful even when you were ill-tempered, cynical and faithless.

Child, I showed patience with you as your healing progressed. Will you do the same for another whose heart is darkened and confused?

I do not require that you compromise the truth. All I require is that you continue to *live* in truth.

Then you will speak the truth in love, as My Spirit enlightens the eyes of your heart to see as I do. I love you.

Yours With Deepest Trust,
Dad

THE SIMPLE TRUTH
John 3:35; 6:37-40; I Cor. 6:7-12

*C*herished but Angry One,

You can hate your way out of your inheritance, but you cannot hate your way out of My love. It just cannot happen. My love led you into My arms, and it will lead you back into them again. It is only a matter of time.

Meanwhile, you cannot reign in Our Kingdom of light as long as you allow the tyranny of darkness to reign over you. Resentment is gross darkness! It will never establish the glad government of Heaven's True Light in a chaotic world wracked with pain.

This warning has nothing to do with My depriving you of your reigning position, treasured one. It has everything to do with *your* abdicating your throne and allowing bitterness to ascend and take charge. That is the simple truth.

I care about your pain, and I love you with all of My heart. I cry with you. Will you draw near and allow Me to hold you? This burden is too heavy for you.

Your Strong Refuge Always,
Father

I HAVEN'T LOST MY TOUCH
Heb. 2:9-18

*S*orrowful One,

Why do you cry? I have already shown you how Kingdom policy requires that eternal gains often first appear as losses. Don't despair. You will only have to return to hope if you do. Consider Christ! He defeated death, but He conquered by yielding, not by resisting. When the world's Savior, beaten and bleeding, hung in agony on His cross, no one could foresee His victory.

His loved ones could feel only horror and stifled outrage for His humiliation as they beheld His anguish. When they gazed upon their mutilated Messiah, all they could see was disaster... searing pain... injustice... the gross wickedness of corrupt human government... dying dreams. But were they right? Did they see the whole picture? You know the answer to that. Tearful child, always remember: Christ's submitting to His cross portrays perfectly the way of My wisdom, for it shows that in Heaven's economy death detonates a surge of Divine Life.

So when My wisdom is at work, things usually appear worse before they look better. It was the same with Abraham and Sarah as they awaited the birth of their son, Isaac, was it not? It was. They died to their dream of bearing a son. Years later, Isaac's son Jacob was tricked into marrying Leah and forced to postpone his marriage to Rachel for yet another seven years. Jacob's favorite son, Joseph, tasted a similar and perhaps a deeper sorrow. His dream bit the dust when his own brothers sold him into slavery.

Do you think young Joseph thought his imprisonment in Egypt even faintly resembled a promotion? Hardly! I heard him quietly sobbing himself to sleep many nights, so I should know. Nevertheless, Joseph rose to be second in command over all Egypt. He became the king's most trusted counselor and the deliverer of multitudes of people. Joseph also became the redeemer of his family—including his brothers who had abused and betrayed him.

I AM the God of Abraham, Isaac, and Jacob; and as with Joseph, I still turn imprisonments into promotions. I haven't lost My touch! Your own life fully demonstrates this fact. I know your pain. Again, your dreams are suffering violence, treasured one. But in the roar of that violence you can hear the low rumble of Resurrection Power resurging—if you will become quiet and listen.

Tenderly,
Father

SKYDIVING
Prov. 3:5-6

esitant Conqueror,

It's like skydiving. Leaping out of an airplane from 10,000 feet above the earth is not easy—but it is fun! And that's putting it mildly. *Exhilarating* is a better word, as any seasoned skydiver will tell you.

Selling all you have, or better yet, giving it all away to follow Christ is like skydiving. The same is true when it comes to heeding My gentle heart-whisper and daring to step out (seemingly into nowhere!) in obedience.

Do you know why some people become sullen, critical, negative, hard to live with? They are bored! That is why. I built them for adventure, not boredom, and their spirits are restless to soar. Can you relate?

I know that some of your loved ones and fellow workers have trouble understanding you. Even so, I like you whether or not you are easy to live with! Besides, I know you will obey Me sooner or later. Why are you waiting?

Yours With All Power, Always!
Father

OUR AT-ONE-MENT
I Sam. 17:47; Col. 1:15-23

*T*rusted Liberator,

You have yet to obey Me in this, but I'll keep harping on it anyway. Cease fretting about yourself! Cease worrying about My battles. They are Mine, are they not? Believe in your Anointing. I do! I have always trusted My Holy Spirit. You *are* making progress. These days it is becoming more difficult for you to wallow in the mire of doubt. I have noticed that, and I know that you have noticed it too. You are beginning to enjoy living in trust.

Good! That is because of Our at-one-ment. You live in Christ and He lives in Me. Is there a more secure place where you could be? I hardly think so! In time, not only will you think as I think, you also will feel as I feel. You will know with deepest assurance that I love you and that you are Mine.

Yet what has made it so difficult for you to live in trust? I will tell you. Beneath the surface of back-breaking self-effort lurks the suspicion that evil packs more power than good. That suspicion is what fuels the paranoia that empowers all legalistic systems, many of which advertise themselves as proclaimers of Christ. Amazing, isn't it? But it is true. Many of My unwitting children strive, struggle, and strain to achieve victory, yet they live in despair and pain. It has not dawned on them that through Christ's cross I have granted them victory. I have abolished sin once and for all!

What is good? Why is it stronger than evil? In your Lord's opinion there is only One Who qualifies to be called Good—the very One Who speaks to you now. Yes, Good happens to be Who I AM. Good is not a what, but a Who! So how can any evil, however fiercely entrenched, outlast Almighty God?

Slow down, calm down, settle down. Choose to trust the Good Light Who lives inside you. Decide again to rely on the still, small voice that leads you. I will not leave unfinished the work I have begun in you. I did *not* devise My own defeat when I created you, dear child. What would have been the point?

Yours With Unfailing Commitment,
Father

P.S. Do not allow anyone or any influence to remove you from the hope of this wonderful news I have shared with you! It is sheer joy having you in My life. I delight to constantly present you spotless in *My* sight. So please do not deny Me that joy by struggling to appear righteous in the sight of others. Many thanks!

TRYING TOO HARD
Mark 4:30-32; I Cor. 12:14-27

*W*eary One,

I delight in diversity, don't you? Our Kingdom is like a tiny seed. When it is planted, it grows into a massive tree—resilient, lush, and vibrant. Birds of every variety alight in its branches and enjoy rest and a sense of safety and belonging.

The world's kingdom despises diversity. Its tree springs from a synthetic seed, believe it or not. However, it does give birth to a tree that is large and lovely to behold, if lethal to life and variety. (This season the seed is available mainly in pastels, as I recall.) This artificial wonder spawns a tree that sprouts silicone branches of near-perfect symmetry, laden with fruit that is large and decorative—and inedible.

Many, many fowls of a banal sameness flock to its foliage. They all look alike, flap their wings alike, lay eggs alike, chirp alike, build nests alike, hop alike, and sing alike. They even go through the ritual of mating alike! Though, oddly, they seem incapable of mating for life. Even so, these creatures do exhibit remarkable qualities. For example, they can instantly vaporize into nonexistence when decreed to be "out of fashion." Then, as if on cue, they can flash into re-existence, all of them sporting *this* year's colors and plumage.

Child, I know it seems a "fowl" thing to ask...nevertheless, My heart for you compels Me to pose a question. Of the two trees I have described, which do you find more inviting? I will let you sow another silicone seed and grow another look-alike tree, if that is what you want. But are you sure the world's befuddled birds will flock in great numbers to roost on its branches? Bear in mind that the branches of your tree will be identical to the ones they are already sitting on elsewhere.

I think you are trying too hard to fit in. When will you choose to enjoy just being the delight I have made you to be? One can waste a lifetime, striving to conform to a "norm" held by a fictitious majority that simply could not care less. I love you as you are! Your uniqueness is what makes you special to Me. I mean that.

Love Always,
Dad

istracted Child,

Thank you in advance for being kind to yourself! Feeding a fantasy only fuels lust and expands its capacities so that nothing can satisfy it. Are you aware that another word for lust is *covetousness*? Covetousness spawns all kinds of evil. It unravels the rationality of all who allow it to rule. It empties bank accounts, fills hospitals and mortuaries, destroys dreams, erodes trust, and breaks hearts. And that is not all; a lust-driven life renders *authentic* relationships impossible. I know you, child. That is *not* what you want out of life.

In Christ My grace has appeared in the world to teach and to train everyone how to say "no" to evil and how to say "yes" to Real Life—how to relish Real Life! Some people wrongly imagine that because I AM Love, that means I do not allow consequences. That is a lie, cherished one. I AM Reality Personified, as I have told you before. That means *unreality* that destroys people is *not* welcome in Our universe.

Do you know what would be the most unkind thing I could do to you or to anyone else? It would be to let abuse that calls itself "love" forever have its way with Our world. That definitely applies to spiritual abuse. It also applies to physical abuse of every variety. I will not—indeed, I cannot—allow evil to devour My cherished creation. It is not going to happen. I intend to make all things new! Our enemy's days are numbered. The tyranny of sin and death *will* come to an end. I love you. That is why I tell you the truth.

I want Us to co-labor in establishing Love's dominion worldwide! If you choose not to reign with Me and opt to establish your own kingdom instead, I will still love you with all of My heart. Furthermore, I will not be your Enemy. But you need to know that you will have become *My* enemy—Love's enemy. I AM kind to My opponents, of course. That is, insofar as they will allow Me to be. However, I will *not* ensure their safety or happiness at any cost. Sooner or later all who persist in using other people to satisfy their own selfish agendas discover that...*I AM a Consuming Fire.*

Long ago an ambitious angel started a rumor. Do you recall? He accused his Creator of being the ultimate "Killjoy." My first human children believed him. Do you believe him? I honestly don't think you do—not in your deepest heart. You know by experience that I AM your Fountain of Joy.

Please understand that it is not My intention to offend you, treasured one. My intention is to keep you on track with Reality. Your highest good is My deepest desire, and you know that. You and I both know that!

Yours With Unceasing Devotion,
Father

ZAP!
Ps. 31:23-24; II Cor. 4:3-6,9-12

*W*eary Restorer,

How right you are! Criticism nearly always comes at a bad time. Just when you are juggling a thousand crystal goblets and breaking your neck to do everything right—*zap!* Like a swift arrow shot out of the ozone, a sharp word from a faultfinder pierces your heart. "Why do you always...?" wheedles the voice. Or worse, your detractor announces, "God has given me a word for you!" Sound familiar? You forget that I hear all conversations, don't you!

Moving on... A prime time for a wet blanket to smother your fire is when you are most earnestly seeking to do My bidding. It occurs when you are *pouring out your very life* to love and serve others. It happens when you are doing your gut-wrenching best. It is then that those pompous little nitpickers appear out of nowhere and sweetly intone, "May I say something in love?"

Then, when with trembling hands and heart you smile back and mumble, "Uh, yes, please do," of course you know what is coming. And you guessed it right! You find yourself weighed in the balance and found wanting. It is a pattern nearly as predictable as sunrise and sunset.

All you have to be doing is your very best! Then suddenly, from his lofty height of piety, a self-appointed purger will swoop down and pounce on you and box your ears! You can count on it. Those critical spirits do lie in wait, just looking for opportunities to sabotage your joy. What seems worse is that I allow them to come.

And why? For one thing, I don't think you laugh enough. I want you to develop a robust sense of humor, and that will happen as you learn not to take yourself too seriously. Furthermore, I want you to find your deepest joy in My approval. The more you realize the fleeting nature of human approval, the more you will appreciate Mine.

Child, you will never rest, nor will you ever learn humility, until you *know* that your value has nothing to do with your abilities. Your value is infinite because you belong to Infinite Love! Period. The end. Full stop!

I AM proud to report that one good thing is already surfacing in your personality. These days you nearly always think twice before you dispense *your* advice. I AM so pleased to see Christ's character forming in you!

Last, but not least... I will never send any messenger to you who implies that I demand that you love Me more than I love you. People—or even angels—who convey such irrational messages are self-sent. You can be sure of that. The message, "God is Love, *but*..." is a lie.

Yours With Joy Everlasting,
Father

AS MY LOVE HEALS
II Cor. 5:17-21

*S*earching One,

You died in Christ and were raised with Him. His life swallows up your death. Therefore, you are to judge no one by the flesh—by external appearance—and that includes yourself. But you've forgotten that, haven't you? Never fear. My tender care will cure you.

More and more you will find yourself saying "no" to sin and "yes" to Real Life. I only ask that you receive My forgiveness when you stumble and return to My loving nurture. That is because Unconditional Love is Who I AM. Therefore I show you kindness and lavish you with gifts, even when you avoid My Presence. I know that the love-seeds I AM sowing into your life will yield a harvest of holiness. Be assured, all of your old self-defeating habits will vanish as My Love heals and transforms your heart.

Already, when you look at your fellow human beings, you are noticing changes in the way you perceive them, aren't you? It is becoming increasingly difficult for you to covet any pleasure that would bring destruction and heartache to another person.

Covenant keeping... self-restraint... these qualities characterize Caring Love, and they *will* abound in you.

With Joy!
Your Committed Father

DISCOVERY
Rom. 8:17-18

aring Deliverer,

When you made up your mind to allow My Spirit to lead you, you didn't foresee this time of testing. I saw it coming, but you did not. I knew you would experience losses. I knew you would struggle though long, howling deserts of silence. I foresaw the pressures that would bombard you from without and the pain that would fester from within.

However, it was when the hard times came that you realized the cost of heeding My gentle prompting. It was then that you also discovered the strength of My commitment—and yours. Only fiery trials can evoke such discovery.

Child, I want to thank you for not giving up. You have not been rebellious or proud, but you *have* been stubborn. But I love your kind of bullheadedness! You have not been flawless, but you have been faithful. If it were not so, I would tell you.

Some people have challenged your motives; others have questioned your sanity. Even you have wrestled with uncertainty over these issues, many times! I was glad you did. Never once did I become annoyed about it. I saw the fruit that all the furor was producing in you! The challenges strengthened, the questions clarified, the pressures purified—and I AM satisfied. And you are fortified! Now We can begin the adventure!

Yours Proudly,
Father

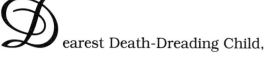

HOME
Hos. 13:14; Luke 3:1-6; I Cor. 15:55

earest Death-Dreading Child,

It happened in about three seconds. The victim sensed only a sharp twinge of coolness, a numb impact as the floor rushed into his face, a fleeting ache mingled with swirling images—then oblivion.

John found himself on his feet, staring in silence. He watched a swordsman seize the bleeding head by its matted hair and plop it onto a large platter, which he shoved into the hands of a subordinate.

Despite his cool demeanor, the eyes of the younger soldier widened slightly, registering shock and disgust. "Somebody's got to do it!" retorted the older, wiping and resheathing his saber. The two strode out, bearing their gruesome trophy. Never once did they look behind them.

With calm detachment John watched the armored figures mounting the stairs that led into the darkness beyond. What was that mad music and revelry blaring in the distance? Was Herod hosting another party? Whatever it was, it hushed with the slam of another door.

John glanced around the cell. His eyes fell on the mutilated body that lay half kneeling, half sprawling at his feet. *Where am I?* John wondered. *And who was this man judged deserving of a death so brutal?*

"You are with Me now," came a Vibrant Whisper. "You are beholding the remains of My voice in the wilderness, a man willing to decrease so that I might increase. Do you remember?"

Joy surged, and John remembered. Then he forgot.

That is, he rapidly began forgetting as gentle beings, emitting lightning radiance, appeared and surrounded him. Moments later he noticed their loving arms were somehow nudging him higher. Awestruck, John realized that he and his welcoming party were ascending stairs that spiraled ever upward into a life-transmitting radiance that no earthly tongue could describe.

Why have I never noticed these stairs before? John thought to himself.

As he rose into the brilliance that showered from above him, music unknown to mortal ears ravished him with unspeakable joy. The higher he ascended, the more it swelled with unbearable sweetness. Earth-memories vanished amidst the music...

What else mattered? John was home.

Yours at All Times and in All Worlds,
Your Loving Father

I CAN DEAL WITH THAT
Acts 2:18

earest Daughter,

I think you should know that many people open their hearts to you who have yet to know how to open them to men. You live in a fatherless generation, cherished one. So I AM anointing you to raise up many sons who will grow up to become true fathers in Our household.

What do you think? I think I have called you! That is what I think. So I will vindicate you and open doors for you that *no one* can shut. My prophet Joel foretold that My "handmaidens" also would prophesy. I intend to fulfill that promise. Of that you can be sure.

I know you feel unworthy, little one. I can deal with that easily enough. If you considered yourself qualified, believe Me, I would be sending you an entirely different message!

Seeing you smile always delights Me ...

Stop worrying about satan's devices, chosen daughter. No, I did not make a mistake; I refuse to capitalize Our enemy's name! Of course you realize that I have no desire to insult him; it simply has always been My policy to lift up the humble and to put the proud in their place. You have observed Me do that many times, haven't you!

It is error to think of satan as being the "sheer personification of evil." Evil is merely a perversion of goodness. So how could it have the substance required to be a person? Our enemy is a person because I created him *before* he grew wicked. Oh yes, he now does evil, but evil is not his real substance. Actually, satan possesses only one virtue—albeit a sadly tarnished one. He is very industrious! He is not at all lazy.

Would you like to demolish his schemes? Ignore him and sing for joy! That will do it every time.

I believe in you!

With All of My Heart,
Your Dad

AN OPEN MIND
Deut. 4:29; I Cor. 13

*L*ovable Explorer,

Hmmm... So you have decided to approach the question of My existence with an open mind, have you? I think you should know that you are not reading these words by accident.

To be honest, ever since you decided to abandon your "faith," I have had mixed feelings. On one hand, because your earlier perceptions of Me were so muddled (and far too religious!), I was glad to see you discard them. On the other hand, I have sorrowed for your loneliness. Having no God and believing in a false god, in the end, are equally stressful for a being created to enjoy the True and Living God.

However, I have had no choice but to honor *your* choices—at least for a season. Had I interrupted your search prematurely, you would have acknowledged Me and related to Me, but only after a fashion. In many respects you would have remained frustrated and imprisoned.

You certainly would not have known the depth My love will descend to help you, which you now know by experience.

Are you annoyed that I have suddenly shown up? Please don't be. I cannot hide forever behind the scenes. Treasured child, you live in My universe and *you* are an important part of it. So of course I think about you all the time!

I have "overheard" you thinking about your needing a new beginning. I was not trying to meddle; knowing everyone's thoughts just happens to be a natural "limitation" of My Omniscience. However, I think you should know that I want a new beginning for you even more than you do. I long to help you avoid another false start and to provide you with a real one.

I AM available to help you anytime you wish. I just want to let you know that.

Your Best Friend,
Father God

P.S. I remember hearing you pray recently when you found yourself in a "tight spot." Who were you talking to?

PACKED WITH MEANING
Rom. 5:5; Heb. 13:8

*S*truggling Son,

Think for a few moments about the miracles your Lord performed in His earthly ministry. He opened deaf ears and blind eyes, caused lame legs to walk, and cured people of leprosy. My Son even raised the dead!

All of His miracles are packed with meaning. Have you ever thought about their implications? When He restored crippled limbs, Christ exhibited My power to heal that which is lame in the human personality— your personality. By opening blind eyes He demonstrated My ability to give sight to the eyes of your heart. Even now, chosen conqueror, He rends the veil that blocks your vision of Who I AM and of Who I AM for you! In the Light of Who I AM, you will discover who you are. You then will see *and know* your true identity and purpose. I promise you, son! Soon the beauty of things you have not yet beheld in their true glory will ravish you. You will see them from My perspective! Then, things you once found attractive will grow dull in your eyes.

You will wonder how they ever enticed you. That which is deaf in your deepest heart will flourish with sensitivity. That which leads to nowhere and is leprous and degrading in your affections will fade away like a forgotten dream.

Christ makes all things new. Yes, out of nonexistence He calls forth new desires and affections, for He is the Resurrection and the Life. And He is *your* Strong Deliverer. You have not misplaced your trust!

That is, not until recently... Lately, you have hindered Heaven's good work by trying to help. Tell Me, what caused you to commence that strenuous behavioral modification program? You are becoming so rigid and tense that your loved ones can hardly live with you—let alone enjoy your company!

Son, what you desire cannot be manufactured, for it is not humanly concocted. What you seek is a miracle that only Christ in you can perform! He is My Gift of Righteousness to you, and He lives inside you. So be assured, your Lord's childlike virtue will continue to surface in your character. Your heart will be exactly like His! Your life will be exactly like His. That is your destiny. Be at peace about your public image. I AM! I have you covered by grace. Those who trust Christ will not be put to shame. I have given you My word about that, have I not? You know I have. Cease striving and strategizing, and then your agony will cease.

What do I want from you? I long for you to let Me hold you in My embrace until you know—beyond all question—that I love you. When My Living Presence permeates your wounded heart with that certainty, you will have crossed a frontier from which there is no return.

Yours With Unfailing Commitment,
At All Times and in All Realms,
Father

STAND YOUR GROUND
Ps. 24:1; Phil. 4:4-9

 erplexed Pioneer,

Of course Our enemy is agitated! You are invading his turf—or so he imagines! You are taking territory he has dominated for centuries and daring to challenge his claims. Stand your ground. It is *Our* ground.

I AM honoring your prayers. Thank you for trying the untried. I appreciate your refusal to conform to the so-called norms of sterile religiosity. Your courage to reveal My true heart to a hurting world *will* bear fruit. Move forward, cherished one! Refuse to retreat! Rejoice in My unfailing mercy every step of the way. Let no criticism crush your hope. Allow no bitterness to steal your joy.

I have established you in the realization that you can *always* count on Me—no matter what. Rest in that realization.

Child, as experience has shown you, I do not know how to fail! Christ's blood—His very life—covers you. My Spirit anoints, indwells and empowers you. Let love govern your heart, and you will never lack wisdom. Moreover, fear will never find a foothold in your mind.

What you want others to do to you, do the same to them. That is My policy. I always love My neighbors as Myself. I realize that many teachers of religion say I do not, but their traditions have blinded them to Who I AM. That is why I have called you, chosen one. You will show the world Who I AM—Love that *never* fails. Sing for joy!

Yours With Strength Everlasting,
Father

WAYS AND MEANS
Ps. 131; Acts 16:16-29

ressured Conqueror,

Thanksgiving paves the way for peace to return and resume governing your heart. Remember and rejoice in what I *have* done for you. That will free you from torment. I want you to be happy! You may as well be, for I intend to fulfill My promises.

"What has happened?" you have asked. I will tell you. You have sought to live by mere logic, and now you are getting locked into logistics. However, that is nothing new where you are concerned, is it? Never fear! The obsession to reason your way through problems, apart from listening to My Spirit who dwells inside you, will not always dominate your life. I can assure you of that!

Even so, at the moment, a "rational" devil that fosters irrational behavior continues to gnaw away at your nerves. He would love to reason you right out of your mind! Are you going to let him? You don't have to if you don't want to, cherished one. Instead, you can remember and relish the miracles I have already performed for you. Will you do it? Think thankful thoughts. Sing for joy, and I will sing with you! I have ways and means of dealing with problems that you cannot begin to imagine.

Thanksgiving will release your spirit to receive fresh revelation and new insight. Enter in! I AM already singing—

Joyfully Over You!
Dad

A WILLING HEART
Ps. 62:12; II Cor. 8:12

xhausted Child,

You have not been selfish. Your gifts have been most generous. What a blessing you are! Cease condemning yourself. I said it long ago, but I will say it again: Yours is a willing heart, so I honor your gifts on the basis of what you have, not on the basis of what you lack. This policy applies whether your gifts be financial or whether they simply consist of your labors of love. When are you going to realize I AM not a Pharisee?

Oh yes, I will indeed judge—and reward—all my children according to their works, yourself included. But aren't you glad that it is I who will do the judging? When I judge, mercy multiplies. When people judge... But you already know how that turns out, don't you? Always, always I look at motives. I examine hearts. While We're on the subjects of hearts, will you now allow Me to sort out some things that have been happening in your own? Don't be afraid, treasured child. Relief! That is what I have in mind for you.

I have caused you to cling to Me. It is not by your own might that you press into My Presence. I have drawn you to Myself. Why? I long to mend your heart with the healing warmth of Mine. I intend to exchange your ill-fitting, ragtag clothes for radiant glory-attire befitting your royal position. I AM going to throw a party for you!

Yours, Already Celebrating,
Father

LEARN THE SECRET
Ps. 16:5-6; Heb. 5:14; Rev. 3:7

herished Child,

I have already promised to bless all of earth's families in Christ. That includes you and your family as well. So you must not allow false responsibility and worry to drive you into enterprises that I have not ordained for you. When My children buck against the boundaries I have established for them, they sabotage their own success. So please bear in mind that I open doors that no man can close, and I close doors that no man can open.

When through Scripture I told you to make the most of every opportunity, I was referring to those opportunities that I clearly provide. It was not in My heart for you to receive those words as a mandate to launch into a mad scramble to renovate the world overnight. You must learn the secret of waiting—especially at this stage of your growth, cherished one. But yes, you are right. Lately I have been reining you in and frustrating your plans, which are worthy enough, but untimely. Please do not blame others for hindering your ministry. The blame, as it were, is Mine.

I love you too much to lose you to religiosity. That cruel treadmill would only bring you heartache and exhaustion. As I have told you, I have a "champagne taste" regarding your destiny.

Yours Patiently,
Your Loving Father

MY UNCONDITIONAL LOVE
Ps. 130; Matt. 5:38-48

earest Daughter,

Bear in mind that love looks for ways to believe the best about others. Love does not delight in exposing sin, nor does it rejoice when another fails. If I kept a record of wrongs, who could possibly stand? But My heart is a forgiving one. That is why you treasure Me and hold Me in highest esteem. I so appreciate that. You keep telling others how My unconditional love has healed you and freed you to live in hope. And it is true, isn't it? I have won your deepest admiration because I have loved you no matter what you did or did not do. It is My kindness that has led you to repentance—miraculous transformation in your thoughts and behavior, your very life.

Do you yearn for others to respect and love you? I know you do, cherished one. So throw away your list of infractions! Forgive those who have hurt you and choose to forget their failures. In this way you will overcome evil with good.

No human being can thwart the wonderful plans I have for you. Trust My relentless love. Hope in My power! In Me there is *full* restoration, and I will always rescue you from every evil device. You have no reason to worry. Do you see it, little one? Your future and that of your loved ones does not depend on man. I AM your Provider, your Protector, your Promoter, your Almighty Father and Closest Friend. Your future depends on Me! Many thanks for your trust!

Loving You Always,
Dad

NABBING NITPICKERS
Ps. 18:25-29; 94:12-15; Matt. 7:1-4

*H*arassed Child,

When carping words come to wound and discourage you, bear in mind that I will defend you. I always see to it that people who lay down the law to others are themselves laid low by the law. Oh yes, of that you can be sure! I make certain that they entangle themselves in their own talk, sooner or later. What else can I do? I have no choice! It is just the way things work in the Kingdom of Heaven. It is a spiritual principle. It is not that I particularly enjoy nabbing nitpickers and outmaneuvering manipulators. But who else knows the rules well enough to outwit them—to show them reality? You certainly do not. Furthermore, I don't expect you be your own defense attorney!

Let Me work the rules! Trust Me to vindicate you. I have proven Myself able, have I not? As you well know, your Good Shepherd and I have interesting ways of tenderizing the hearts of hardheaded people. We even know how to make them happy while We do so!

Do you recall how Heaven's Blazing Light nabbed Saul of Tarsus? In a single moment your Lord reduced that opinionated rebel to a quivering heap at His feet! Saul became known as Paul thereafter. Moreover, he became one of Heaven's most notable friends. As Paul himself would tell you, I AM extremely resourceful!

Your Mighty Fortress Always,
Dad

THANK YOU
Luke 10:10-37; Gal. 6:1-2

*F*aithful One,

I want to thank you for supporting My weaker child. I have seen your many hours of constant caring and how you have devoted your time and substance. Oh yes. I have known when others have not. Time and again I have watched as, with agonizing effort, you have forgotten your own sorrow and labored on to comfort another who is confused and badly broken. So again, thank you. You have been a friend—and My friend—in the truest sense of the word. Please know I will not forget your sacrifices. How could I?

Yes, I know. Certain ones who should know better (yet who prefer to remain at a comfortable distance) have hinted that your labors of love could ruin your reputation. It has even been sweetly suggested that people might identify you with the shame of sins not your own. And some who are far holier (?) than I AM have denounced your efforts, saying your work has brought dishonor to Christ...

However, your Lord and I have discussed these things at great length, and He doesn't have a clue of what they're talking about! On the other hand, We both know *exactly* what your critics are talking about—and it is not about you. It is about them. Of course, they have yet to realize it.

Just remember, your reputation will stand or fall with Mine. So why worry about it? So what if We have become "of no reputation"? Tenderhearted one, I have gone this route before, believe Me, and there is nothing like a timely resurrection to revive a tarnished reputation! Be of good cheer. All the clamor and commotion will cease with the grand promotion I have planned for you.

Then you will discover how many friends you have had all along, won't you? Yes, you'll have yet another opportunity to forgive and forget, but join the club! I do it all the time.

> With All of My Heart,
> Yours Proudly,
> Abba Father

A BEASTLY REVELATION
Num. 22:21-31; Book of Jonah

eliberating Conqueror,

Balaam the prophet was so bent on doing his own thing that when his donkey began talking to him, he did not even notice the incongruity. He retorted instantly, as if conversing with an animal were an event as normal as scratching his nose! Poor Balaam. He was so obsessed with his plans that he could not detect the oddity of this remarkable occurrence or experience any sense of wonder. The man was too blind to see the sun in the sky. Far less could he perceive that he had lost touch with the Spirit of revelation and that I had anointed his worthy beast instead! Alas, such is the nature of greed: *Ambitious minds always miss miracles.*

Jonah had a similar problem. He too was My prophet, but he got it in his mind that he was more spiritual than Yours Truly. When I commissioned him to warn the Ninevites of My coming judgment, he knew I would spare them if they repented. So he balked! Jonah had no love for the people I yearned to save. Moreover, he preferred to enjoy the approval of his biased peers over having Mine. So he tried to run away. My beloved but stubborn prophet flatly rejected My call.

So? I found a vessel that *would* respond—a fine and frolicsome fish! As you know, I have never had a problem with animals. Those noble and pure creatures, from the least to the greatest, all delight to do My bidding. I have commissioned cows to transport My Covenant Ark. I have inspired frogs, locusts and flies to change the mind of a proud king. The fish I sent to swallow up my prejudiced prophet Jonah also did an excellent job of persuasion. Do you recall?

I know this has been a "beastly" revelation, in a manner of speaking. However, I just thought it would be good to remind you that I can anoint anyone or anything I choose. Furthermore, all that I desire to occur *will* come to pass. Whatever I purpose *will* happen.

Thank you for refusing to compromise your calling. Thank you for not striving to fulfill the agendas of religious people who are shortsighted and selfish. I appreciate your choosing to walk the path of love—no matter what the cost. Thank you for doing what I have called you to do and for being who I have called you to be. Yes, treasured one, I realize that I AM thanking you in advance for your obedience. However, as I recall, you often thank Me in advance for answering your prayers, don't you? I love Our transparent relationship.

Love Always,
Your Omnipotent Father

IMPERFECT PEOPLE
Eph. 4:1-16

*M*y Valiant Defender,

Sometimes I subject your ears to voices expounding doubtful doctrines. Do you know why? I appoint imperfect people as Heaven's demolition agents to explode the illusion of perfectionism and to irritate those who promote it. Perfectionism hinders true holiness.

Each time idolatry of intellect makes love with pride of appearance, another devil (accuser!) is born. I allow imperfect people to bungle about in Our house so that laughter can render such cohabitation ridiculous! Holy mirth dismantles pride, leaving idolatry without a lover.

By the way, I have also missed hearing your joy-generating wisecracks. I mean that.

Yours Entreatingly,
Father

YOUR CLOSEST FRIEND
Ps. 139; John 3:16-17

ear Truth-Seeker,

Never underestimate My ingenuity! I have ways of showing up in your life that would boggle your mind. You have demanded that I prove My existence and My love for you. I have no intention of letting that demand go unchallenged.

But of course! You can count on it. I always act and respond in ways that you could never foresee. I love to surprise you. That is why My friends who know Me heart-to-heart find Me interesting, believe it or not. However, you tend to think of Me as being dreary and dull. I don't blame you for that. The pompous little god that joyless religiosity advertises bores Me too! Since your understanding of Who I AM came from that source, I could not agree with you more. The idea of "God" that you (thus far) have acquired truly is dreary and dull.

Angry? Why should I be angry? Many of My children have a muddled perception of Me. It would be absurd to take personal offense in their case or in yours. People can only know what they know. That is, until I show up!

You have wondered about hell... *Hell* is a word that means "grave." I AM Love Personified. From My point of view, people who do not know Me do not know Love. They are dead—spiritually dead. They are in *grave* condition. When people refuse the Light of My Love, I must allow them to remain in spiritual death—as long as they prefer it. Of course, that doesn't mean I give up on them. After all, I sent My Son into the world to raise the dead!

Have I ever given up on you? Certainly not! I know the pain that festers inside you and how it is rooted in your wrong perception of Who I AM. I just want you to know that I AM available and that I AM your Closest Friend. So you can enjoy My company anytime you wish. Only dare to become quiet, and listen to your heart.

Not one moment passes that I do not think of you. Not one! Soon I will confirm this fact by a small miracle of supply. You will not be able to explain the arrival of this gift in any other way than that I dropped it "out of the sky."

What a wonderful smile you have! I like it.

Yours Respectfully,
Your Real Dad

SOUNDING OFF
Ps. 86:9-13

ear Child,

Here I AM again! It delights Me to show up for you at just the right times. I know My sudden appearances often surprise you, and I AM also aware how they sometimes irk you.

I don't always seem interested in the issues you would like to address, do I? Instead, I begin sounding off about My dreams for you; or about repentance; or of the need to forgive others; or about the benefits of patience, commitment, trust—you name it! I show up out of the blue and begin talking about anything and everything but the topic you have in mind.

Cherished one, I regret that My ways annoy you on occasions. If it pleases you, you can attribute them to My old age. I have been around for a very long time! However, you have another option. You might ask yourself *why* the issues that consume all of your attention seem more important to you than what I have to say...

Yes, in a sense you are right. In a manner of speaking, I AM turning your little world upside down at the moment. Actually, I AM doing you a favor. I AM destroying a false world and giving you a real one! Once the dust settles, I think you will be greatly relieved.

Simplicity... order... sanity... a solid sense of significance and purpose... You have yearned for these, have you not? Yes, and I have yearned even more that you have them. Your pain matters to Me. *You* matter to Me, far more than you can imagine.

Thank You for Trusting,
Dad

WHATEVER HAPPENS
Ps. 103:3; Isa. 53:4-5; Heb. 13:8

uestioning Child,

When I first confirmed to you that your prayers had reached My ears, I knew you would need additional encouragement later on. Don't worry about symptoms! What appears to you as your difficulty returning is actually the reverse. The affliction is no longer working its way inside of you. Now it is working its way out.

Sing for joy! Delight in Me, cherished conqueror, as I delight in you. Cease analyzing and scrutinizing that which is on its way out; plunge into your new life, and enjoy!

You may as well take the plunge now, for—whatever happens—I *will* complete all I have begun in you. So why not choose to be happy? I AM!

Loving You With Fierce Devotion,
Father

OUR TASK
Rom. 12:1-2; 1 Cor. 6:9-20

$\mathcal{R}$ecovering Restorer,

You already know this, but I will tell you again. I oppose promiscuity that calls itself "freedom" because I know that it is *not* freedom; it is bondage. I know the heartache it brings.

I AM Unfailing Love, true enough, and I AM glad you realize that. Even so, I cannot be a responsible Father and at the same time cancel all negative consequences in Our universe. Often I can modify them, and in My mercy I do so. Yet even then many of My children reap a harvest of untold agony simply because they have ignored *Reality.*

Please, treasured child, make it easy on yourself and on My tender heart for you. Do anything wholesome and fun, but flee fornication! I want you to enjoy your life! Living in lust will render that impossible, sooner or later. It will cause *real* happiness to elude you. Giving free rein to your passions will only bring you pain and regret.

Yes, I will confirm ... The lights have come on, so to speak. Child, you are now seeing that most of your mental anguish has been self-imposed. So Our task is to retrain your brain, isn't it? As astonishing as it seems, I can even make sure that you have *fun* while I renew your mind. That is because your thought patterns heal and your cravings change as you learn the simple joy of walking and talking with Me. In other words, your restoration will come as I impart increasing revelation to your heart.

More and more I will show you Who I AM, who you are, and what Our lives are all about. Not only will I show you these things, I also will cause them to become *solid realities* in your deepest being. Furthermore, I will impart many kinds of miraculous knowledge to your spirit, the details of which will astound you! They also will amaze other people. Through your life they will experience My wisdom and Presence and become envious to know Me as you do. Follow Me, and you will love everyone from a pure heart. I will see to that. Furthermore, I will protect you from people and influences that would seek to exploit and hurt you, and I will provide for you. Haven't I always? I have already provided you with a new life! I have rescued you from religiosity. As a result, you now know beyond all doubt that I AM committed to you.

That is wonderful to know, isn't it? Thank you for listening.

Loving You Always,
Father

NOTHING TO LOSE
Zeph. 2:11; John 5:22-23

*C*hosen Liberator,

Rejoice! There is nothing to fear. You must not confuse mere appearances with realities. I AM now answering the heart-cry of all who yearn for deliverance. As you recall, Christ is My Healing Light, and He is committed to shine on all who weep in darkness. That is why the world's totems are toppling and corrupt religious systems are crumbling. These are not catastrophes, child. They are indicators of the Light of My Glory increasing worldwide!

As the bogus gods of earth and their lying illusions disintegrate, people begin searching for the True and Living God. This describes your own experience, does it not? The time came when you "lost" everything, including your reputation. Then you decided to trust Me with your public image. You also chose to rely on Me for your provision. So now you have nothing to lose. Isn't that wonderful? No earthly care can oppress you because, at last, you have a life!

As chaotic as circumstances appear, My Radiant Redeemer Son—as never before—is infusing *life* into the world. Do you recall that I have committed all judgment into your Good Shepherd's hands? I have done that, not to destroy My lost sheep, but to restore them. It is time that they become all that I have longed for them to be. The world-weary *will* come to their senses. When they do, they will deeply honor and adore your Lord and Myself for Our kindness in freeing them from their destroyers. They will no longer cherish the idols that only brought them pain.

Child, you now are free. Things no longer possess you. People's opinions no longer rob you of sleep. Hasn't that caused you to love Me all the more? Indeed it has. Surely you know that your increased devotion has not escaped My notice!

That is why it has been My delight to empower *you* as never before to infuse life into Our world—to shatter the shackles of despair. My Light shines through you and from you with amazing energy that heals broken hearts.

Just remember that you cannot expect to transmit My Spirit's power and go unchallenged. Increased power is bound to stir up even more opposition. That is the simple reality of reigning in Our Kingdom. At least, at present it is. But didn't I hear you say that you wanted to be in the midst of the action? I AM certain I heard you say so—more than once. Well, here you are!

Why not be at peace about it and enjoy Our work together? I AM!

Forever Yours,
Father

LOVE'S ENERGY
Ps. 24:1; Isa. 42; 61; Mic. 6:8; Matt. 7:3-5

rusted Conqueror,

I share your concerns. Any parrot of average intelligence can learn to squawk words. You and I also have observed that some clever humans can learn to wrangle over words and their meanings. However, We both know that mere rhetoric and logic are powerless to heal hurting people. It matters not how well one can "prove" his or her reasoning by persuasive arguments. It matters not how much one may saturate his or her message with Scripture—*words **alone** cannot heal.*

It is My power—Love's Energy—that spawns new creations! Principles, formulas, and instructions cannot raise the dead! That is why I did not send a textbook into the world; I sent My Son. He came to heal the brokenhearted! He did *not* come to explain to them how to heal themselves in 666 easy steps—that actually are *not* so easy. I AM tired of "How to Do It" seminars, aren't you?

Anyone can expose error. Anyone can point an accusing finger. But where are My deliverers? Where are those who *possess My power* to heal and restore? If I seem angry, that is because I AM. I AM unhappy with smug-sounding semantics that reek of the refuse of self-righteousness while parading themselves as "the gospel." I AM heartbroken because many of My chosen co-heirs have no clue as to why I have called them out of darkness into My Marvelous Light. I have anointed them to be a royal priesthood to intercede for a lost world. I yearn for them to transmit My Power—Love's Power! Only *that* will cause the tyrannical governments seated in hell's gates to tremble!

Heaven have mercy (and it does!), I have not called out an "Us-Four-and-No-More-Going-to-Heaven" club to abuse a hurting world with the lie of conditional love! No, I have called out a healing family of co-regents who will not fail or give up until deliverance is established in the earth! The earth is Mine in all of its fullness—*and* those who dwell in it. And it is yours, cherished conqueror. Oh yes, I do mean that. The world is yours for the taking, if you want it.

Do you yearn to see Love fill everything and everyone everywhere? Then go! Set the captives free! I live inside you. My Son Light illuminates your path. You are filled with Love's Energy, so you *will* go in My Power, be assured!

Only bear in mind that reigning with Christ means nurturing, healing, and serving. Cherished one, that means you will suffer. You will suffer, especially at the hands of people who are in charge of controlling religious systems. However, that will remind you that reigning with Christ *does not* mean "lording it over" those whom I have called you to love and heal. A lost and deluded world reigns by intimidation and control, yes. The same is true of a lost and deluded church! But of course, everyone knows that. What else is new? Child, just remember that I have called *you* to conquer by Love—Love that never fails! And thus you will conquer, for Unfailing Love is Who I AM.

What a joy it is having you in My life! I mean that.

Your Devoted Father

hosen Deliverer,

I don't mind telling you again. Any thought that destroys your hope does not come from Me. Please remember that you are not in a position to properly assess your success. Your destiny is to live in revelation, not to be locked into mere information. That is why I tell you that you must not judge anything or anyone by outward appearance—including yourself.

Righteous judgment almost never bears even a faint resemblance to the conclusions that human beings reach by natural reasoning. The truth—the whole truth—contains too many factors for the mortal mind to grasp. For example, in your limited vision the earth appears flat. However, We both know it is round. Even so, it looks flat because your physical eyes can perceive only a small part of the whole. The same holds true for your view of success. Believe Me, if I suddenly caused your life to conform to your present concept of success, you would not be pleased at all. Have you forgotten? I know you! I know you better than you know yourself.

So it all comes back to trusting in Me, doesn't it? You have read in My Word that nothing less than childlike faith can please Me, and that is true. Yet, here is another thought for you to consider: Doubt and unbelief make *you* impossible to please. (Your loved ones will be happy to confirm this if you ask them.)

Now, just to encourage you ... I know that you have thought your recent prayers were selfish and vain, but they were not. Not only did you pray in harmony with My will, My Spirit empowered and inspired your petitions. Consider them granted! Soon you will discover that My range of interests far exceeds what you have always imagined. I think it is time to begin broadening your thinking.

Yours With Joy,
Dad

P.S. Keep this message a secret, will you? Some of My children are too steeped in religious tradition to appreciate My policies at present.

MY COMMITMENTS
Isa. 46:9-10; Matt. 5:38-48; 22:39

*H*urting Child,

You need to know that I *never* give advice that I do not follow Myself. Nor do I command anything that I cannot carry out in My own Life. I will never require something of you that I Myself do not possess. Little one, that would make Me worse, by far, than a hypocrite. Such a contradiction in My character would make Me a lunatic! How could I teach others what I do not know?

You are not wrong to disbelieve in the irrational god of man-made religion. Those who believe in him (it!) become irrational themselves. My commands are My commitments. They are what I Myself commit to uphold. Bearing this in mind, consider what the following commands/commitments say about Me:

- What you would have others do to you, do also to them.
- Be angry and sin not.
- Do not let the sun go down on your wrath.
- Give cheerfully!
- Always forgive, even if it comes to forgiving 70 x 7 times—daily!
- Be thankful in all things.
- Love your enemies, and bless those who curse you.
- Refuse to return evil for evil, but instead overcome evil with good.

Cherished one, I AM hoping that as you ponder these commands, you will realize that they are a description of Who I AM. Christ came not to contradict, but to fulfill the law and the prophets. These are summed up in the words, "You shall love your neighbor as yourself." Aren't you His little neighbor?

Loving You Always,
Father

BEAR WITH ME
Matt. 6:25-34; Eph. 3:20

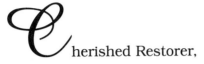herished Restorer,

I know you better than you know yourself. What you think you want is often different from what you truly want in your heart of hearts. That is why, as your Loving Father, I must exercise sound judgment and at times seem to disregard some of your requests. Actually, I AM not ignoring your desires. As experience has already taught you, I AM working to grant your *deepest* heart-longings.

It is your real needs that matter in the long run. Don't you agree? I AM considering your real needs even now in response to some of your prayers for promotion. I hope you'll not mind My asking, but are you ready for this change you seek? It is not wise to judge by the outward appearance of things. A baby bear appears cuddly and winsome, and he is—when he is a mere cub. Living with him after he has grown up is a different matter! But I AM sure you already know that. We both love animals, don't We? So, I know you will "bear" with Me as I reassure you of My good intentions for your future.

Hmmm... A "more dignified public image"... You aren't serious about wanting that, are you? Living up to an image has never satisfied you before. You are too hopelessly real for that! We both know that you are *still* too down-to-earth for that. I know you. Have you forgotten? I formed you!

Calm down, treasured child. Allow Me to help you have a fresh look at your life and your deepest aspirations and calling. Lately you have drifted out of touch with *yourself*—your true self, that is. How do you expect Me to fulfill your requests when you have no clue of what you are talking about?

I Love You!
Dad

*W*restling Warrior,

You must learn not to speculate about My opinions without first inquiring of Me. How would you feel if you stood among your friends and they theorized and talked about you as though you were absent? Would your heart ache if they deliberated and devised how to spend your money? What if they kept piping up about what they thought you might desire or think, and it never occurred to them to ask *you* personally? That is how most of the Church treats Me.

They come together for what they call a "prayer meeting" or a "service," and what a strange event it is! My friends mindlessly turn to Me and parrot a few memorized words and clichés. But after that? They conduct themselves as though I were nonexistent!

Is it any wonder that most church meetings bore Me? To say nothing of boring My intimate friends who know Me as a Real Person! Such rigmarole not only bores them; it grieves them. It grieves them even more than it does Me. But that is just how close friends are with each other, isn't it? I would much prefer that someone hurt Me rather than one of My friends. And, of course, that is how My friends feel when people dishonor Me. I know you can relate to what I AM saying.

Cherished one, you keep asking that I become more real to you. May I tell you a secret? When you begin treating Me as a Real Person, you will discover—beyond all doubt—that I AM a Real Person. However, as long as you do all of the talking and none of the listening, I will always seem unreal to you.

Dare to quiet your heart, dear child, and listen more often. Cease theorizing, speculating, and reasoning. I AM ever present. Allow Me to be Myself.

I have missed your company.

Your Devoted Father

*V*aliant Savior,

You indeed are a co-savior and co-heir with Christ. However, you are not *the* Savior. You are a co-laborer with Him. Isn't that a relief to know? I AM your Diligent Father and the Manager of the cosmos. I AM above all, through all, and in all. I *work* above all, through all, and in all. So give yourself a break, child. Please... give all of Us a break! You are not in control. I AM. In this truth you must rest—and rejoice and be glad. I AM a Restorer. With all due humility, I AM the Restorer above all restorers. I never begin a work that I do not bring to breathtaking, glorious perfection. Never!

Again, child, any thought that tortures your mind and prods you into frantic self-reliance does *not* come from My Spirit. Any thought that drains away hope comes from Our enemy. I allow challenges to arise in your life to deepen your trust, not to harass or hurt you. So cheer up! We—you and I—are on the right track. Furthermore, We are on schedule. Your loved one is also on schedule—exactly.

So why do I often keep you in the tilt position? It is so that you will lean on Me, of course! I AM training you to rest in hope, for it is in such repose that you *experience* the Joy-radiant Life that is your portion.

As for the wisdom you have sought... Yes! Request granted. Consider it done! I have told you this before, but I don't mind telling you again. Be honest. Be gracious also. Let your yes be yes and your no be no.

Keep it just that simple! Gently yet firmly refuse to yield to seduction or unrighteous compromise. Always seek to transmit caring love, and you will never stray far from wisdom. I will see to that.

Thank you for taking time for Us! I love you.

> With All of My Heart,
> Your Omnipotent Father

MY KIND OF HOLINESS
Matt. 5:42-48; I Cor. 3:10-23

*H*arassed Deliverer,

Your friends do not love you for how holy you look or for how attractive, rich or successful you are. They love you because you are you. Child, they love the person I have made you to be. Would you be happy with friends who loved you for any other reason? Of course not. So why fret about the fleeting opinions of people who don't even know you?

You are My temple, My house. I live inside you. Simply rely on Me, and the radiance of My holiness will shine from you. I have not called you to earn brownie points or to keep up appearances. I detest such straw spirituality! Many traditions that legalists esteem as sacred, I regard as refuse! I AM looking for hearts that will reflect the Light of Christ, My Self-Giving Son. His is My kind of holiness. It is the kind that appears "unholy" to somber sobersides who care only about appearances.

So you want to be perfect, do you? Wonderful! Then do what I do. Shower healing grace on imperfect people. Pour your heart out to love the disreputable-looking ones in Our world. Comfort the outcasts. Be friends with the nobodies. Nurture and restore those who fail. Help heal the abused—as well as their imprisoned abusers. Cherish and honor people whom a sanctimonious church and a hard-nosed world care nothing about. Hold them in your arms. Cry with them. Love and assist them *always*—even if you never see your prayers for their healing answered in this lifetime.

Then—and only then—will you begin to be perfect as I AM. Thank you for resigning from the religious rat race.

I Love You!
Father

I KNOW WHERE WE ARE GOING
Ps. 18:25-29

*R*estless One,

Shhh! Settle down. Quiet your heart. Trust Me. I know where We are going. I have promised to protect you. I will shield you from all harm, never fear. Just make yourself at home in My Presence. I AM your Defense, so be assured—all accusations will come to naught, and all opposition will vanish.

Meanwhile, savor the true tranquility that comes when you take refuge in Me. Why do you imagine that I AM reluctant to help you? It is not in My nature to give grudgingly. I delight to support you! I realize that I seem "slow" from your point of view. And yes, you are right. I never fret about time. As you well know, I AM a Shrewd Strategist, and I do have surprising ways of rearranging schedules. Have you noted how I have rearranged yours? I even made time for you to receive this brief message, didn't I?

I AM smiling with you!

Dad

Recovering Conqueror,

Even now Our ministry is touching many people you will never meet until death fades forever in the unrelenting light of True Life. Rest assured! All who received life-transforming hope through your loving labors will come to thank you in their appointed time. They will cover you with kisses and weep for joy for having the honor at last of meeting you personally.

I know you still wrestle with sorrow. You think that if only you had tried harder, all those days of chaos would not have come. Perhaps so, if you had tried harder, cherished one. But you did not. And why? Because you could not! You gave everything you had. If anyone knows that, I do. And believe it or not, *I* rejoice for all that you have given and done!

Will you please hear My heart? I AM not angry. I AM not disappointed in you, nor am I punishing you. I AM preparing you. I AM restoring and refurbishing you for a ministry that is far greater than the one you have accomplished thus far.

Do you recall those tearful times when you pleaded with Me to empower you to resist the dark forces that relentlessly tortured your mind? I do. Cherished one, at this very moment I AM answering your prayers. Of course, I AM only telling you what you already know. This is but a confirmation of what you are now experiencing.

Just keep looking to Me. If certain ones cast a critical eye your way, what is that to Us? It doesn't matter. Unhappy people infected by joyless judgmentalism will be powerless to hurt you if only you will keep your eyes—your attention and focus—on Me.

Thank you for allowing Me to lead you along a painful path. It was a necessary one, and now you can see why. Others whom I have placed in your life also can see why. It is gloriously evident to all whom you touch that your journey into despair was for *their* blessing.

You have no idea how much joy you bring to My heart.

Your Devoted Father

ARE YOU INTERESTED?
Isa. 40:31; John 14:12; I Cor. 1:9

L oving Liberator,

Learn to rely on My wisdom and leading. I long to help hurting people, just as you do. However, grief sometimes rages in human hearts with such mind-binding intensity that words (any words—good, bad, or indifferent) tend only to increase their torment. More often than not, your loving presence and silent prayers supply all that is needed.

Who you are... What a magnificent gift! You, child, are a healing light to many wounded hearts, though you do not see or know how. If it were not true, believe Me, I would not say so. My Spirit dwells inside you! Shouldn't I know the Gift that I AM in you?

One day you will prophesy with astounding accuracy! You will possess power to open blind eyes and deaf ears. Furthermore, you will be able to heal crippled people, cure the hopelessly insane, raise the dead—and even renovate worlds! You will know how to be in one place and then suddenly appear in another. The weather will change at your command. You will even be able to walk on water.

You will consistently tell the truth, and always love and forgive others. Moreover, you will always understand and appreciate My thoughts and respond to My voice—without fail! And according to Jesus, your Lord, you will do even greater works than He did. Glories await you that no mortal eye can see, no natural ear can hear, and no finite mind can imagine!

Are you interested? Spend more time with Me.

Your Unfailing Fountain of Joy,
Father

YOUR HIGHEST GOOD
Eph. 1:1-11; Rev. 3:14-16; 5:5

uestioning Child,

You are right. I show up when I please and I disappear when I please! I do *exactly* what I want to do — all of the time. The same is true of My Spirit, who moves like the wind, and of My Son, the Lion of Judah. And while We're on the subject of lions...

I enjoy cats of all kinds, have you noticed? People tend to love them or hate them. There is almost no middle ground in the way human beings respond to felines. Some find them annoying; others find them delightful. However, nearly everyone agrees that those clever creatures seem independent and proud.

Shall I, as they say, "let the cat out of the bag"? I think I deserve at least the same treatment that people give to the common house cat. Love Me or hate Me! I mean that. I prefer being disliked over being patronized — anytime!

Child, why should I not come and go as I please? Where were you when I designed the blueprint for the galaxies? In My heart, of course; that's where you were! You were nestled in there with My deepest affections. Your highest good will be forever at the heart of My actions, My policies, My comings and goings.

Never fear! I do have limits. Have you ever thought about that? Perfect Love *must* do what It wants. That is because Love always wants the very best for the ones whom It cherishes. Aren't you glad?

I AM not as far away as you think.

With Deepest Devotion,
Your Real Dad

AN ASTRONOMICAL NUMBER
Ps. 22; 66; 96; Rev. 4:11; 5:13

9 nquiring Child,

Am I ever depressed? Funny that you should ask. To answer that question, I think I should remind you that I deal with an astronomical number of factors and issues. At all times and in all realms—past, present, and future—I oversee and sustain multiple billions of people, worlds, and creatures. At every moment I care for them individually, and at every moment I also care for them corporately.

Never fear, cherished one; such labor never depresses Me. I perform these functions as easily as a man might wiggle his toes in his sleep! One could say that I manage Our multi-dimensional cosmos by instinct. I AM not aware of any effort involved. That is, I never feel any stress from My work. So, in an overall sense, I never experience depression. Wouldn't We all be in deep trouble if I did? I cannot be anything less than Almighty God, because I simply AM What and Who I AM—All Pervading Joy, Unfailing Holy Love.

However, at times some situations do sadden a part of My heart. For example, I grieve for the deception and pain of people who refuse to receive My love. My heart aches when My wayward children recognize truth yet choose to build their lives on lies. I weep also for all who are abused, afraid or lonely, burdened or suffering.

May I be utterly honest? Sometimes your depression does depress Me a bit, so to speak. For example, you and I enjoy an intimacy that My prophets of old would have envied. As a result, you live in a constant flow of miracles! How is it, then, that you still harbor the fear that I might abandon or betray you?

Child, as I have told you before, that thought never crosses My mind—not until you bring it up on occasions. When you trot that wretched nonsense before Me, I will admit, I grieve. I sorrow—especially for you. Have I loved you so long, yet you know Me so little?

Repentance acknowledged. Now forgive yourself!

Forever in Joy,
Your Devoted Father

GOOD IDEAS
Isa. 55:6-9; Acts 16:11-38; I Cor. 1:20-31

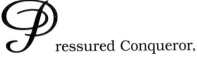ressured Conqueror,

Don't let the "facts" deceive you. Those facts that your limited mind can perceive are only bits and pieces. The truth, the ultimate and total reality, is too vast for your physical brain to compute, little one. It is so important that you learn to follow My Spirit and not rely on your own natural reasoning.

At the moment I AM allowing you to face many issues in order to train you to trust My still, small voice. I know your circumstances are hard. I understand that you wrestle with difficult choices. I AM aware of the pressures that weigh you down. I have also chuckled as I have watched you daydreaming and devising ingenious routes of escape. No doubt about it, you do concoct some interesting plans!

Why are you afraid to trust My Anointing? What makes you so sure of your own rational processes? Do the factors in this situation *really* furnish you with sufficient data to justify your conclusions? Beware of good ideas. Ishmael was a good idea. King Saul had many good ideas.

You need more than common sense today—and every day, for that matter. You need My wisdom! My wisdom boggles the minds of the astute of this world. I empower adolescent poets to topple giants with slingshots. I grant donkeys vision to behold angels and anoint them with astonishing wisdom to prophesy. I once healed a man's leprosy by instructing him to bathe in a river that was by no means pollution-free. I have even been known to rain bread from the open sky!

And I like doing things "backwards." For example, I delight to cure blindness by applying mud to the eyes of My patient, so that at first it appears I have rendered him doubly sightless. Nothing pleases Me more than confounding the minds of those who take pride in their own common sense! Thus My wisdom often tends to reveal itself in the far-fetched, the outlandish.

Speaking of the outlandish... Who would have ever conceived of My commissioning a fish to carry a gold coin in its mouth for tax time? Is it logical to talk in terms of taking a leisurely stroll *on* the lake? Your Lord viewed such excursions as business as usual. And His views exactly reflect Mine.

You have asked for My opinion, so here it is: Some of your plans look a little too "logical" for My tastes. Wait for My wisdom! It is My delight to help you! Cutting through mountains of red tape is My specialty. Do you remember how I once freed Paul and Silas from prison? The folks at Philippi of Macedonia talked about that little shakedown for years...

Truly!
Your Devoted Father

YOU'D BE BORED
Matt. 5:9; Acts 3:21-23

elightful Deliverer,

Whatever happened to your sense of humor? I miss your chuckles, your corny wisecracks. I really do. Do you know why I appointed you to this post? I brought you here to act as a "buffer zone" between the bullheaded and the belligerent because I knew you were accustomed to being caught in the middle. In fact, I trained and toughened you all of your life to be the nurturing peacemaker you are.

Why? Somebody has to do it. Besides, I know you. You'd be bored with a "normal" environment. If I didn't toss you into trouble you'd go looking for it yourself. I AM sure you won't argue that point!

No, I AM not annoyed. I AM proud of you! You've done a better job than you think. I just want you to recover perspective. Your ministry can be an exhausting enterprise, granted. However, peacemakers like yourself *are* the restorers who will bring about the restoration of all things that all of My prophets have foretold!

I empower My caught-in-the-middle children to work mightier miracles because they face pressures that My other children do not. But you sometimes forget this truth, don't you? I don't mind refreshing your memory and granting you wisdom. I AM your Father, and that is My job. Ask, and you shall receive ...

I love seeing you smile.

Your Almighty Father

FOR A MOMENT
Ps. 34:8-10

herished One,

Are you lonely? Depressed? Bored? I think you are. That is why I have maneuvered you into this place to calm and quiet you. Do you think I AM selfish? Some people think I AM. I just want you to know that I miss you and that it saddens Me to see you struggle alone. I thought I would remind you of how much I love you and of how important you are in My life. You are where you are now for only this reason.

I AM so happy! Now you are Mine—entirely, if but for a moment. And I AM yours, child, just for the asking.

Always,
Father

INTO THE JET STREAM
I Thess. 5:18; I John 4:17

*W*eary One,

If you don't mind, We can address what you would like to talk about later. And I promise you, We will! At the moment, however, I would like to talk about thankfulness. I AM so grateful for all your efforts to show it, especially considering all the "unexpecteds" that have recently come your way.

I just want to encourage you to remain focused on My faithfulness—not on negative factors or people. As you know, these are destined to change! No, treasured warrior. I AM not being sarcastic. You *have* shown gratitude. I realize that you've not done it with flawless consistency, but you have tried! You need to know that I know that.

You also need to know that your obedience has thrust you into the jet stream of My highest aspirations for you—to say nothing of My promised provision! And I intend to keep you there. Only bear in mind that you should not expect the world to give what it does not possess. Refuse to harbor resentment toward lost people, for that only confirms to Our enemy that his tactics to distract you are working.

Why give him the satisfaction? Jesus Christ is the Perfect Picture of Myself that I sent to your world. As Perfect Love in human form, He came to show human beings what I have destined *them* to become!

The wounded of Our world need to be *introduced* to Christ. The only way they can be saved—experience wholeness—is to receive the Healing Son of My Love. They need to become familiar with His essence, to savor His fragrance, to *experience* His transforming touch. Otherwise they will continue searching for Love along paths that lead only to pain. My lost sheep do have an instinct that prods them to search for their Good Shepherd. Yet unless He reveals Himself, how will they ever find Him?

Trusted child, you know Jesus Christ! He lives inside you. You've got the Picture! *Show* hurting people— as well as abusive people—what He is like. I AM not asking you to prepare Bible studies. Not that I AM opposed to such endeavors, of course. But you have been asking for a return to simplicity, have you not? Request granted!

Love Always,
Dad

*M*y Treasured Ambassador,

Go! Go in the assurance that I have you covered. Forsake all morbid self-scrutiny. Instead of focusing on your flaws, think of Us and choose to relish Our relationship. Then it will not be your frailties that others will see. They will behold My Light of Life radiating from your presence—Christ in you, the Unfailing Hope of Glory!

I repeat, child, do not fret. It is not going to happen— not ever! I will not let you come to dishonor. Nor will I permit your trust in Me to leave you humiliated and desolate. As you well know, I AM faithful. I may not be predictable, but I AM always reliable. Furthermore, chosen one, My reliability has nothing to do with your track record! It has everything to do with My passionate love for you.

I know rest is hard work for you. At least, at this stage of your life it is. However, it is *only* a stage that you are experiencing, I assure you. Will you believe Me? I AM gently leading you ever upward into imperishable joy. I AM causing you to ascend from one level of glory to another. I AM raising you from one exhilarating height of My grace to another. Therefore, rest *will* come. After all, it is your inheritance. As you go, you will know!

I have already given you eyes to behold other people as I see them and a heart to love them as I love them. How it delights Me to send you forth to be the blessing I have made you to be!

And just for the record, you are *not* an inconvenience. Almighty God being inconvenienced ... hmmm ... amazing thought, that one! I love your sense of humor.

Dad

HEART TO HEART
Isa. 49:2-4; John 14:21-23; Eph. 3:10-12

*R*estless Child,

I AM with you. I confirmed this fact only moments before now. However, your hunch is correct. These days I speak to you less often through other voices. You know why, don't you? I AM helping you to grow up!

As long as you look to others and to the outward appearance of things around you instead of listening to your heart, you will never know the joy of knowing Me literally and personally. A deep undercurrent of restlessness will run inside you. You will not be happy because I created you to commune directly with Me, heart-to-heart.

But yes. You are on the right track. Furthermore, all is forgiven, just as I have told you, cherished conqueror. I have lavished you with wisdom for all situations. Therefore you are fully equipped for all that lies ahead!

Cease searching for signs and get on with fulfilling your high calling! I have given you many signs. What would you do with more? Carry on! Trust in My integrity. I will keep My promise to direct and protect you. Have I not proven Myself? You know I have.

I AM promoting you—as of today. If I left you in spiritual kindergarten it would reflect poorly on Me. That is, unless I established you there as a teacher. Is that what you want? Now? I think not. I know you better than that!

Yours Joyfully,
Dad

TIME FOR US
Ps. 90; 111:10

ense Conqueror,

At last! Now you are doing the very thing I have longed for you to do. You are taking time for Us. Wonderful!

What! You think I pressured you to arrive at this point? Why should I bother, when you are such an expert at pressuring yourself?

Recently one of My sons attended his thirtieth-year class reunion. There he saw the woman for whom he had sworn years before that he would curl up and die unless I consented to make her his wife. She had grown older than her years, as well as become coarse, sour, cynical — and *loud*. Even worse, throughout the whole evening she showered her gracious and gentle husband with whimsical demands and unkind words.

Was My son ever relieved that I had refused to grant his earlier requests! Would you believe that he is still dogging My tracks and thanking Me? Consider!

I realize that dealing with delays is one of your less developed gifts. And you've guessed it right. These days I AM allowing you to experience delays more often. However, My letting you wait is not to annoy you, chosen one. I AM conditioning you to appreciate My strategies while you enjoy Heaven's serenity. Exciting, isn't it?

Yours With Deepest Devotion,
Father

THE MIND OF CHRIST
Mark 4:35-41; I Cor. 2:16; Phil. 2:5-13

*S*truggling Conqueror,

Again, you must test all things and hold fast to that which is good. Do the thoughts bombarding your mind at this moment enhance your hope in Me? Or do they foster unceasing analysis, confusion, and worry? My dear child, there are many truths. However, My Spirit will not lead you to focus on any truth that does not free you to hope in My power and love. My highest priority is that you live constantly in the mind of Christ—His mentality, His servant-hearted love, His childlike faith, His unshakable serenity.

You have the mind of Christ. My Conquering Son dwells inside you. Decide now to abide in His peace that defies reason and transcends understanding. Mere facts will never free you to relish the abundant life that I have prepared for you. At the end of the day, it isn't what you know that counts. What counts is Who you know! Of course, that does not mean I want you to adopt a policy of refusing to deal with the realities of life. What it does mean is that I want you to remember afresh that Unfailing Love is the Ultimate Reality that governs all other realities. Armed with that knowledge, no fact, however real or true, can erode your joy.

Your Lord once commanded a storm to cease that rose on the Sea of Galilee. The winds were real, the waves were real, the threat was real. It was a "true" storm. It just was not as true as I AM! Your Savior knew that. That is why He could sleep in the back of a small boat that rose and plunged amidst watery wave-mountains while His cherished disciples were frantic. That is exactly how I want you to think, feel, and behave. Any thought that renders that kind of tranquility impossible *does not* come from My Spirit.

I appreciate your trust.

Yours With All Power, Forever,
Dad

Postscript

Do you know your heavenly Father—personally? Or do you just know about Him? Have you ever heard Him chuckle, or congratulate you or tell you He loves you? Has He ever comforted you, or given you miraculous and sudden bursts of insight—revealing knowledge otherwise unobtainable? Do you have conversations with your heavenly Father? Do you ask Him questions? Do you hear Him telling you "yes" or "no," or giving you timely words of counsel? Have you come to know Him as a warm, loving, all-wise, and all-powerful "Dad"? The Bible teaches that our Father really wants each of us to know Him in that way.

The Bible is God's perfect love letter to us. He sent us that love letter to lead us to Jesus Christ, our Father's greatest Gift to our world. And Jesus came to show us His Father and to *demonstrate* how we should relate to Him. He literally conversed with His Father all the time! Jesus knew the Scriptures, but He also knew the God of the Scriptures—intimately. Christ used the eyes and ears of His heart and was led by the Holy Spirit. He declared that He did only what He "saw" His Father doing and spoke only what He "heard" His Father saying. And here is the real shock: Jesus told *us* to do as He did! In fact, He created us to enjoy *real* conversations with the *real* and *living* God.

When you think about it, the whole reason Jesus came, lived, died, and rose again was to make possible that kind of relationship with our Dad. Christ wants us to be walking, talking miracle-workers who hear the voice of our Father and enact His tactics to liberate hurting people. We have been chosen to be co-rulers with Almighty God—forever! It all begins now, but planet Earth is only our training ground.

Sound incredible? It is! The mere thought of our destiny is so awesome, it jolts our limited intelligence systems into "thermal overload." Our call is too grand and too vast for our small minds to compute; but it is true.

If all this sounds foreign to you, too far-flung, but somehow strangely captivating, I invite you to join me in the following prayer. Pray it aloud:

"Heavenly Father, I want to know You in a real way—a personal way—just like Jesus did. I realize that You sent Your only Son, Jesus Christ, into this world to make that possible. He died on the cross for my sins and was raised to life by the power of Your Spirit. Now I commit all that I am to Jesus' care—to His Lordship. Your Word says that if I confess Jesus as Lord, I will become Your child, Your heir. I decide now to believe that promise and receive Jesus as my Lord.

"Thank You for honoring Your Word and adopting me into Your family. I know I can trust You. And Father, please lead me to some of Your older children. Send me among men and women who already talk to You and hear You talking to them. I want to learn from them. Protect me from those who are "religious" but deny Your power to speak today, and keep me from any other influence that would hinder my relationship with You.

"In Jesus' name, Amen."

Take this opportunity to affirm this life-changing transaction by your own written testimony:

On this _____ day of _____ , in the year of our Lord _____ , I, _____ , entered into a covenant relationship with my heavenly Father. I yielded my life to the Lordship of Jesus Christ, and by the promise of my loving Father, I now belong to Him forever. I hereby consent for my God to exercise His full parental prerogatives on my behalf. Henceforth I will look to Him to be my Dad and will trust Him to keep my tomorrows.

(signed) _____

Scriptures to strengthen your faith:

John 1:12; 3:16	God promises eternal life.
John 5:39	The Scriptures lead us to Christ.
John 5:19,30	Christ hears the voice of His Father.
John 14:12	We, too, can hear our Father's voice.
Isaiah 55:1-3,10,11	Our Father longs to commune with us.
Matthew 7:7-11	Our Father will talk to us if we ask.
James 1:5	Our Father will give us His wisdom.
Romans 8:14-15	Abba Father is the name for Dad.
Romans 8:16-17	We reign as co-heirs with Jesus.
John 20:21	Jesus commands us to be miracle-workers, too.

Index

Have you enjoyed the art of

C Hawley

Cliff Hawley has been
ministering with his
inspirational art for more
than 20 years. If you would
like to see more, you can
find him on the internet at
www.chawley.com. To
purchase a print of one of
his pieces from this book or
our others, you can contact
him on-line or by his tollfree
phone number.

- On-line: www.chawley.com
- By phone: 1.800.883.8779

He would love to hear from you!

Other
Destiny Image titles
you will enjoy reading

THE GOD CHASERS (Best-selling **Destiny Image** book)
by Tommy Tenney.
There are those so hungry, so desperate for His Presence, that they become consumed with finding Him. Their longing for Him moves them to do what they would otherwise never do: Chase God. But what does it really mean to chase God? Can He be "caught"? Is there an end to the thirsting of man's soul for Him? Meet Tommy Tenney—God chaser. Join him in his search for God. Follow him as he ignores the maze of religious tradition and finds himself, not chasing God, but to his utter amazement, caught by the One he had chased.
ISBN 0-7684-2016-4

GOD CHASERS DAILY MEDITATION & PERSONAL JOURNAL
by Tommy Tenney.
ISBN 0-7684-2040-7

THE RADICAL CHURCH
by Bryn Jones.
The world of the apostles and the world of today may look a lot different, but there is one thing that has not changed: the need for a radical Church in a degenerate society. We still need a church, a body of people, who will bring a hard-hitting, totally unfamiliar message: Jesus has come to set us free! Bryn Jones of Ansty, Coventry, United Kingdom, an apostolic leader to numerous churches across the world, will challenge your view of what church is and what it is not. Be prepared to learn afresh of the Church that Jesus Christ is building today!
ISBN 0-7684-2022-9

THE RELEASE OF THE HUMAN SPIRIT
by Frank Houston.
Your relationship and walk with the Lord will only go as deep as your spirit is free. Many things "contain" people and keep them in a box—old traditions, wrong thinking, religious mind-sets, emotional hurts, bitterness—the list is endless. A New Zealander by birth and a naturalized Australian citizen, Frank Houston has been jumping out of those "boxes" all his life. For more than 50 years he has been busy living in revival and fulfilling his God-given destiny, regardless of what other people—or even himself—think! In this book you'll discover what it takes to "break out" and find release in the fullness of your Lord. The joy and fulfillment that you will experience will catapult you into a greater and fuller level of living!
ISBN 0-7684-2019-9

Available at your local Christian bookstore.
Internet: http://www.reapernet.com

Other
Destiny Image titles
you will enjoy reading

FROM THE FATHER'S HEART
by Charles Slagle.
This is a beautiful look at the true heart of your heavenly Father. Through these sensitive selections that include short love notes, letters, and prophetic words from God to His children, you will develop the kind of closeness and intimacy with the loving Father that you have always longed for. From words of encouragement and inspiration to words of gentle correction, each letter addresses times that we all experience. For those who diligently seek God, you will recognize Him in these pages.
ISBN 0-914903-82-9

POWER TO SOAR
by Charles Slagle.
With this special pocket book you can enjoy personal notes from the Father's heart every day of the year. Although these lines are short, they have an impact that breathes encouragement into your life...and will almost always make you smile!
ISBN 1-56043-101-6

A HEART FOR GOD
by Charles P. Schmitt.
This powerful book will send you on a 31-day journey with David from brokenness to wholeness. Few men come to God with as many millstones around their necks as David did. Nevertheless, David pressed beyond adversity, sin, and failure into the very forgiveness and deliverance of God. The life of David will bring hope to those bound by generational curses, those born in sin, and those raised in shame. David's life will inspire faith in the hearts of the dysfunctional, the failure-ridden, and the fallen!
ISBN 1-56043-157-1

HINDS' FEET ON HIGH PLACES (Women's Devotional)
by Hannah Hurnard.
What can be more exciting than the *Hinds' Feet on High Places* allegory? It is the allegory along with a daily devotional for women by a woman who has proven her walk with the Lord and her writing gift with other inspirational books. Most of these devotions are "quiet time" meditations, ones that will draw you closer to your Lord Jesus. They will help you to understand your own struggles and regain confidence in your walk with the Lord. This allegory with the devotionals will help satisfy the yearning of your heart. He is challenging you to keep saying "yes" to your Lord as He beckons you on in your own journey to the High Places.
ISBN 0-7684-2035-0

THE DELIGHT OF BEING HIS DAUGHTER
by Dotty Schmitt.
Discover the delight and joy that only being a daughter of God can bring! Dotty Schmitt's humorous and honest anecdotes of her own life and struggles in finding intimacy with God will encourage you in your own personal walk. Now in the pastoral and teaching ministry with her husband Charles at Immanuel's Church in the Washington, D.C. area, Dotty continues to experience and express the joy of following her Father.
ISBN 0-7684-2023-7

Available at your local Christian bookstore.

Internet: http://www.reapernet.com

D *Destiny Image*
New Releases

AUDIENCE OF ONE
by Jeremy and Connie Sinnott.
More than just a book about worship, *Audience of One* will lead you into *experiencing* intimacy and love for the only One who matters—your heavenly Father. Worship leaders and associate pastors themselves, Jeremy and Connie Sinnott have been on a journey of discovering true spiritual worship for years. Then they found a whole new dimension to worship—its passion, intimacy, and love for the Father, your *audience of One.*
ISBN 0-7684-2014-8

ENCOUNTERING THE PRESENCE
by Colin Urquhart.
What is it about Jesus that, when we encounter Him, we are changed? When we encounter the Presence, we encounter the Truth, because Jesus is the Truth. Here Colin Urquhart, best-selling author and pastor in Sussex, England, explains how the Truth changes facts. Do you desire to become more like Jesus? The Truth will set you free!
ISBN 0-7684-2018-0

ENCOUNTERS WITH A SUPERNATURAL GOD
by Jim and Michal Ann Goll.
The Golls know that angels are real. They have firsthand experience with supernatural angelic encounters. In this book you'll read and learn about angels and supernatural manifestations of God's Presence—and the real encounters that both Jim and Michal Ann have had! As the founders of Ministry to the Nations and speakers and teachers, they share that God wants to be intimate friends with His people. Go on an adventure with the Golls and find out if God has a supernatural encounter for you!
ISBN 1-56043-199-7

THE ASCENDED LIFE
by Bernita J. Conway.
A believer does not need to wait until Heaven to experience an intimate relationship with the Lord. When you are born again, your life becomes His, and He pours His life into yours. Here Bernita Conway, the founder and President of International Ministries of Dayspring, Inc., explains from personal study and experience the truth of "abiding in the Vine," the Lord Jesus Christ. When you grasp this understanding and begin to walk in it, it will change your whole life and relationship with your heavenly Father!
ISBN 1-56043-337-X

Available at your local Christian bookstore.

Internet: http://www.reapernet.com

Other *Destiny Image titles* you will enjoy reading

When your heart is yearning for more of Jesus, these books by Don Nori will help!

NO MORE SOUR GRAPES

Who among us wants our children to be free from the struggles we have had to bear? Who among us wants the lives of our children to be full of victory and love for their Lord? Who among us wants the hard-earned lessons from our lives given freely to our children? All these are not only possible, they are also God's will. You can be one of those who share the excitement and joy of seeing your children step into the destiny God has for them. If you answered "yes" to these questions, the pages of this book are full of hope and help for you and others just like you.
ISBN 0-7684-2037-7

THE POWER OF BROKENNESS

Accepting Brokenness is a must for becoming a true vessel of the Lord, and is a stepping-stone to revival in our hearts, our homes, and our churches. Brokenness alone brings us to the wonderful revelation of how deep and great our Lord's mercy really is. Join this companion who leads us through the darkest of nights. Discover the *Power of Brokenness*.
ISBN 1-56043-178-4

THE ANGEL AND THE JUDGMENT

Few understand the power of our judgments—or the aftermath of the words we speak in thoughtless, emotional pain. In this powerful story about a preacher and an angel, you'll see how the heavens respond and how the earth is changed by the words we utter in secret.
ISBN 1-56043-154-7

HIS MANIFEST PRESENCE

This is a passionate look at God's desire for a people with whom He can have intimate fellowship. Not simply a book on worship, it faces our triumphs as well as our sorrows in relation to God's plan for a dwelling place that is splendid in holiness and love.
ISBN 0-914903-48-9
Also available in Spanish.
ISBN 1-56043-079-6

SECRETS OF THE MOST HOLY PLACE

Here is a prophetic parable you will read again and again. The winds of God are blowing, drawing you to His Life within the Veil of the Most Holy Place. There you begin to see as you experience a depth of relationship your heart has yearned for. This book is a living, dynamic experience with God!
ISBN 1-56043-076-1

HOW TO FIND GOD'S LOVE

Here is a heartwarming story about three people who tell their stories of tragedy, fear, and disease, and how God showed them His love in a real way.
ISBN 0-914903-28-4
Also available in Spanish.
ISBN 1-56043-024-9

Available at your local Christian bookstore.

Internet: http://www.reapernet.com